The Contradictions
of Leadership

The Contradictions
of Leadership

A Selection of Speeches by

James F. Oates, Jr.

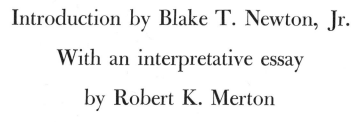

Introduction by Blake T. Newton, Jr.

With an interpretative essay

by Robert K. Merton

Edited by Burton C. Billings

Appleton-Century-Crofts

Educational Division

Meredith Corporation

NEW YORK

Introduction

Blake T. Newton, Jr.

PRESIDENT, INSTITUTE OF

LIFE INSURANCE

This is a volume of selected speeches delivered by James Franklin Oates, Jr., during his more than twelve-year tenure as the chief executive of The Equitable Life Assurance Society of the United States. The speeches are on a variety of subjects and problems, all of which are still timely. More than a public record, they constitute the implicit personal testament of a man as he publicly wrestled with himself in his role as a corporate leader.

One hesitates to ascribe to the expressions of an individual with so many facets and so many strengths a single theme, a single strand, a single summation, and say: "That's it—that's what he stood for." Yet, in these speeches, there is a thread, one worth pursuing. In a word, it is the celebration of the individual human being, his dignity, his rights and privileges, his joys and sorrow, his "sacredness" as a human personality.

To the thoughtful leader, conscious always of his own

v

fallability, man—his needs and his dreams—is the only foundation of substance on which he may build his leadership. This is the lesson of Mr. Oates' thought process, stated again and again in these speeches.

Professor Robert K. Merton, the Columbia University sociologist who has worked closely with The Equitable during Mr. Oates' tenure, has written an interpretative essay on the contradictions which are inherent in leadership. His statement is but another way of expressing the common theme of these speeches.

In my own role as a spokesman for the life insurance community, I have worked with and observed Mr. Oates in *his* role as a spokesman for The Equitable. Consequently, when I was asked to write an introductory note for this volume, I accepted the task as both a privilege and a pleasure. He is a man who has brought a special vision and dignity to our industry, and it is a joy to call him friend.

Perhaps a few introductory comments on the substance of these speeches would not be inappropriate. They fall quite naturally into three groupings according to their respective emphases upon the individual, the organization, and the society.

To lead is to give oneself to others. Among those who lead and those who aspire to lead, this is an assumed condition of leadership. To lead, however, is also to receive from others—to be willing to risk opening oneself to others, to be willing to acknowledge that one has the same human feelings and failings as all others. Giving, alone, and receiving, alone, are arid; in tandem they constitute not only the complete leader but the whole man. It is these two conditions which illuminate the first four speeches as they celebrate the dignity of the individual.

In his years as chief executive of The Equitable, Mr. Oates was the architect of profound human change within the organization. It was done, surely, by redefining objectives, allocating resources, establishing programs, encouraging subordinate managers. But perhaps more important to his goal of attaining a more human corporate environment was the tone he introduced into the organization. The next five speeches exemplify his capacity to translate human values into organizational decisions and his ability to manage change.

Throughout his insurance career Mr. Oates has not only been a thoughtful and creative spokesman for his own company and for the industry, but he has frequently spoken out on concerns within the larger society, especially on problems affecting human welfare. The four speeches on unemployment, "social" capital, the urban crisis, and the population problem illustrate the range of his influence in matters of public policy. It is a matter of record that one of his speeches was a significant stimulus to the industry's so-called billion-dollar pledge to make investments in high-risk inner city areas.

The final paper in the volume was written especially for the 1969 annual meeting of The Institute of Life Insurance. We asked Mr. Oates to reflect on the fundamental nature of the business and to share with us some of his vision of the future. The significance of this document in the thought processes of his successor leaders already seems assured.

I am told that Mr. Oates was informed of the plan to produce this volume only after the editing process was well along. Mr. Burton C. Billings has completed the editorial task with distinction, and his introductory comments to each part of the book will help the reader place the speeches in their respective contexts.

The book not only serves as a retirement gift to Mr. Oates from his Equitable associates, but is an important contribution to the ideology of American business enterprise.

Contents

On December 1, 1969, James F. Oates, Jr., retired as Chairman of the Board and Chief Executive Officer of the Equitable Life Assurance Society of the United States. For the previous twelve and one-half years, Mr. Oates provided distinguished leadership of that organization and, during the period, was a strong influence in the entire industry. That influence was largely exercised through his public words as delivered in approximately 200 speeches. Three of those speeches were delivered under the auspices of the McKinsey Foundation Lecture Series, sponsored by the Columbia University Graduate School of Business, and were published under the title of *Business and Social Change.*

Mr. Oates came to The Equitable from the Peoples Gas, Light and Coke Company in Chicago, which he served as Chairman for nine years. Previously, for nearly twenty-five years, he practiced law in Chicago, latterly as a member of the firm of Sidley, Austin, Burgess and Harper. During World War II, he took a leave of absence from his law firm to serve as Chief, Purchase Policy, Army Ordnance Department, in Washington, D.C.

A native of Evanston, Illinois, Mr. Oates attended Phillips Exeter Academy and served as a Second Lieutenant in the U.S. Army during World War I. He was graduated from Princeton University in 1921 and the Northwestern Law School in 1924.

Mr. Oates continues to serve as a director of The Equitable. In addition, he is on the Boards of Colgate-Palm-

Photo by Fabian Bachrach

olive Co., The Brooklyn Union Gas Co., The First National Bank of Chicago, and the New York Telephone Co. He has long been active in many civic, philanthropic, and educational organizations, including the Committee for Economic Development, the National Industrial Conference Board, the National Urban League, the Life Insurance Medical Research Fund, the American Museum of Natural History. He is a life trustee of Northwestern and a charter trustee of Princeton.

Following his retirement as chief executive of The Equitable, Mr. Oates rejoined his former law firm in Chicago as counsel, and he and Mrs. Oates have reestablished their residence in Lake Forest, Illinois.

The Ambivalence of Organizational Leaders: An Interpretative Essay

Robert K. Merton

GIDDINGS PROFESSOR OF SOCIOLOGY

COLUMBIA UNIVERSITY

Consider the popular imagery of the leader in an organization. For some of the many below him in the hierarchy, he is secure, knowing, decisive, powerful, dynamic, threatening, driving, and altogether remote, acting in clear or obscure ways to affect the future of the organization he leads. At eye level, he is more often seen as filled with troubled doubts as he tries to deal with the ambivalences and contradictions of his status. And if his feet are made of a substance more solid than clay, it is because on his climb to the top and with the aid of those who help hold him there, he has learned to still the doubts, to live with the ambivalences, and to cope with the contradictions of his position.

The abundance of people—and if the leader leads, these must inevitably be called the (not necessarily passive) followers—are not altogether unaware of this complex situation. In the political arena, the daily manifestations of the ambivalences and contradictions which afflict the leader have attained the status of a sportive spectacle; periodically, box scores are presented in the press on the current standings of our eminent political figures as their public decisions delight some strata and alienate others. In other spheres of leadership, too, the contradictions of the position have become public victuals. In the time of most recent turmoil, for example, the leaders of our universities have had to resolve their dilemmas on the front pages of the newspapers. So, too, with our church leaders, as they seek to bottle the fermenting spirit of their flocks. And, as the world stubbornly refuses to shape itself into accord with our proclaimed national purpose, we see our military leaders struggling with the basic conflicts of roles which an objective situation has thrust upon them.

Although many ambivalences of leadership are common to all sorts of organizations—political and economic, religious and academic—this essay will deal primarily with that numerous company of American leaders, the topmost business executives, known, ever since the days of Thorstein Veblen, as captains of industry.

Business—the idea and occasionally the ideal of a more or less private enterprise—has long been a major force in American society. For much of this time, it was ideologized in the American gospel of success and so provided much of the rhetoric and part of the substance of the American dream: "from rags to riches." And if Americans are no longer as convinced as they were forty years ago of the self-evident truth of Cal Coolidge's epigram—"The business of America is business"—recent soundings of public opinion show that they are ever more widely convinced of Ted Sorensen's inverted epigram—"The business of business is America."

Whether it is an organization for business or another purpose, there are only two routes to the top: one from within, the other from without. Each has its particular advantages and handicaps; each produces its own syndrome of ambivalence.

The leader coming from within the organization will tend to know it well: its signal strengths and weaknesses, its style of management and the quality of its managers, its living history and its aspirations, its markets, products and prospects. But perhaps he will know it too well. Friendships and personality clashes have much the same tendency to induce myopia in a leader. And corporate associations of long standing, except in the case of the most detached and widely experienced of managers, have a way of limiting the leader's horizons, of impairing his vision, of restricting his view of possibilities for the future. What has stood the organization in relatively good stead in the past—in terms of organizational goals and of the methods deployed to move toward them— may continue to be carried on. This may be good enough for the immediate if not the longer-run future. But the very value of his intimate knowledge of the past successes of the organization may induce what Veblen unforgettably described as a "trained incapacity": a state of affairs in which one's abilities come to function as inadequacies. Recurrent actions based upon training, skills, and experiences which have been successfully applied

3

in the past result in inappropriate responses *under changed conditions.* Thus, to adopt a barnyard illustration used in this connection by Kenneth Burke, chickens can be readily conditioned to interpret the sound of a bell as a signal for food. The same bell may now be used to summon the trained chickens to their doom as they are assembled to suffer decapitation. As the leader from within adopts organizational measures in keeping with his past experience and employs them under new conditions which are not recognized as *significantly* different, the very soundness of training for the past may lead to maladaptation in the present. In Burke's almost echolalic phrase: "People may be fit by being fit in an unfit fitness." Their past successes incapacitate them for future ones. To move from the barnyard to the railroad yard, on such sand, for one, has the history of the American railroads been written.

The assumed advantages and handicaps of the in-route to the top are typically reversed with the leader coming from outside the organization. He does not know the company in depth. Practically all of his first months, if not years, will be spent in its study—its past performance gauged against its past potentials, the capabilities of its people, material resources, aggregate aspirations. The organization must endure a period of contemplative inaction. But if his lack of firsthand acquaintance with the organization is a defect, it also has its qualities. He brings few built-in biases toward the particular organization and its parts (although he will, of course, inevitably have his own collection of biases grown outside). But having no emotional involvement with the past of the organization, he is—or the more easily can be—capable of opening himself to all kinds of innovative possibilities. He can more readily perceive ideas which may have been floating around the organization for years. He brings, surely, a fresh—not necessarily, a correct—approach to the problems and opportunities of the organization he now leads, and an expertise gained outside the intellectual confinement inherent in every organization. Still, he brings with him from outside no guarantee of success, as is attested by the path of corporate leadership, liberally strewn with the bones of "boy wonders," "financial wizards," and "management geniuses" of all shapes and sizes.

The ambivalences of organizational leadership begin, then, at the beginning. They are found in the route the leader followed to get there, whether from within or from without. They begin with the sum total of his previous organizational experience and with the interaction of his own capability for adaptive growth and all the foibles and creative impulses of the organization he leads.

Regardless of his origin, the newly made leader of the organization soon confronts another ambivalent situation. As leader, it is his obligation to bring to his position a vision of the future, a sense of direction as to where he wants the organization to go. He must obey the further organizational imperative, on pain of failure, of sharing his private vision with the total organization. For vision that is remote from the values and wants of the many around him becomes transformed into self-defeating fantasy. Within these obligations are planted the seeds of several conflicts and ambivalences.

The more sharply the leader defines his vision, the

5

more confident he is of his own role (and vice versa). But in sharpening his vision he has narrowed his options. And in narrowing his options he has limited the number and kind of his subordinates who will, with enthusiasm, perceive and work toward the goals encompassed in that vision. For people who are to release their energies toward the attainment of goals must have a voice and a hand in shaping those goals. They must, in short, have a sense of some mastery over their own destinies. Yet with each slice of power released by the leader—and it is power, *i.e.*, the ability to make something happen, which, in the final analysis and however broadly defined, is the core of leadership—the greater becomes his own condition of uncertainty.

A second kind of conflict is in the offing between the leader who projects his own vision and the organization itself. The more "different" and the more radical that vision happens to be, the greater will be the conflict. For just as the leader comes to his position as the synergistic sum of his experiences, so too he leads an organization which is the synergistic sum of *its* experiences. Indeed, the experiences of the organization will be more deeply ingrained—through its history, traditions, culture, and the sheer inertial structure of all organizational life—than those of any of its individual members. Under such conditions, flexibility in the executive grip may, with only seeming paradox, produce a steadier hand.

Whether his vision is large or small, the leader will want—indeed, will have an emotional need—to shape the organization, to change it, to mold it into a creation which, at least in part, he can claim as his own. Yet, inexorably, he in turn will be shaped, probably without his recognition, by the organization, by its needs, its capabilities, its standards. At some distant time, should he look back, he will be unable to distinguish between the changes he has wrought and the ones which have been wrought in him. "It is a time," wrote Emerson, "when things are in the saddle." Or, to paraphrase a typically Churchillian aphorism: "We shape our organizations and afterwards our organizations shape us." Even the most self-confident of leaders will on occasion find it impossible to disagree.

Another ambivalence confronting the leader is built into the circumstance that although nothing succeeds like success, in organizations increments of success become self-limiting. This means for the leader that the organization will be at one and the same time a continuing source of great pleasure and acute pain. The leader will demand that the organization improve its performance, raise its standards, increase its efficiency. And when, through the objective measurement of the budget or some other device, improvement is discovered and entered into the corporate record, the leader will take great pleasure in it. But to obtain even a tittle of improvement, the leader will find that he must pass through a prolonged period of anguish, during which he feels (and sometimes is) personally responsible for the outcome and, in any case, is held accountable for it. And he will find, too, that unlike an individual who is able to assimilate and use new information for sometimes spectacular improvements in performance, a complex or-

7

ganization functions, for the most part, on precisely the reverse principle: that, after a certain point, as organizational efficiency improves, further improvement becomes increasingly difficult.

Still another ambivalent requirement exacted of the leader calls for him to have pride in his organization, to induce or reinforce the pride of other members of the organization, and still to keep the extent of that collective pride in check. The leader must somehow arrange for that composite of pride that is justified by accomplishment and commitment but, at the same time, he must recognize that pride can become overweening, no longer sustained by continuing accomplishment. This is often expressed in what Theodore Caplow has designated as the "aggrandizement effect": "the upward distortion of an organization's prestige by its own members." Having studied 33 different types of organizations—among them, banks and Skid Row missions, department stores and university departments—he found that members overestimated the prestige of their own organization (as seen by outsiders) eight times as often as they underestimated it. (In judging the prestige of other organizations than their own, people tend to agree.) Now, as Proverbs in the Good Book reminds us in its own brand of organizational sociology: Pride goeth before destruction, and an haughty spirit before a fall. In other words, organizations and their leaders who become happily absorbed in reflecting upon past glories at the expense of providing for new accomplishments are in deep trouble. They come increasingly to live and work in an unreal world of self-induced fantasy. And sooner or later, contact with the world of reality forces the prideful leader and his followers to discover that both utilitarian and moral assets waste away if they are not energetically renewed and extended. For the rest of the social system will not stand still. And so organizations which would move with it must continue to engage in both innovative and adaptive change.

While the leader is concerned, perhaps above all else, with pulling the entire organization to higher levels of performance, he will often be put in the contradictory position of being unable to meet the demands for facilities to provide superior performance by the organization's individual parts. He is presented with a classical dilemma of organizational decision. Deeply committed to the goals of the organization, two or more separate departments are each doing their utmost to serve the best interests of the total organization by maximizing their distinctive kinds of contribution to it. But, often, even typically, maximizing the contribution of one part means limiting the contributions of other parts. One thinks of the bright young men and women attracted to the field of electronic data processing who, were the decision in their domain, would systematize the entire universe overnight. There is, in the striving for organizational excellence—although many hesitate to concede it—a balance to be struck that means curbing the single-minded drive for maximum performance by the component parts. The dilemma of decision can be transcended only by having the distinct parts rise to a concern for the whole. Commitment to the goals of the organization then take precedence over commitment to the goals of the department. All this presents leadership with the geeing-and-hawing which leaves the corporate mule in danger of succumbing to the dead-center obstinacy of noncooperation.

From his relations to his subordinates emerge a variety of other dilemmas, ambivalences, and contradictions for the organizational leader. It is the manager's responsibility, perhaps his very first responsibility, to sustain the people who report to him. He is, in fact as well as in word, "the first assistant of his subordinates." Yet who is to sustain the leader? Granting that topmost leadership is "the loneliest position on earth"—a bit of excusable hyperbole—it is not necessarily so for most organizational leadership; not, that is, under the proper circumstances. Those circumstances have to do, of course, with the kind of support that the subordinates give to their superior in his position of leadership. Turned half-circle and viewed from the position of leadership, this means the degree of confidence which the leader has in each of his subordinates.

There is, in every superior-subordinate relationship, a complex of interactions. At the root of them all, when they are effective interactions, is the confidence or trust that each has in the other. For the ultra-rationalists among us, it comes hard to recognize that in organizational life, the prime ingredient of reciprocal confidence is not competence alone, although the importance of competent performance of roles should not be underrated. It is the first stone on which confidence is built. After all, no one is better situated than subordinates to distinguish between a superior's authentic competence and its mere appearance.

This reminds us that leadership is not so much an attribute of individuals as it is a social transaction between leader and led, a kind of social exchange. And again, though some leaders sense this intuitively, the rest of us must learn it more laboriously. Leaders assist their associates in achieving personal goals by contributing to organizational goals. In exchange, they receive the basic coin of effective leadership: trust, confidence, and respect. You need not be loved to be an effective leader, but you must be respected.

Identifiable social processes produce the respect required for effective leadership. First, respect expressed *by* the leader breeds respect *for* the leader. As he exhibits a concern for the dignity of others in the organizational system and for their shared values and norms, he finds it reciprocated. Second, as has been said, he demonstrates technical competence in performing his own roles. He does not merely talk about competence, he exhibits it. Third, the effective leader is in continuing touch with the germane particulars of what is going on in the human organization. For this, it helps, of course, to be located at strategic nodes in the network of communication that comprise much of every organization. But structural location is not enough. Once situated there, he provides with calculated awareness for two-way communication. He not only lets the other fellow get an occasional word in edgewise; he lets him get a good number of words in straightaway. And the effective leader listens: both to what is said and to what is not said in so many words but is only implied. He allows for both negative and positive feedback. Negative feedback, as a cue to the possibility that, in his plans and actions, he has moved beyond the zone of acceptability for his colleagues and subordinates; positive feedback, as a cue that he has support for his initiating actions.

Fourth—and on this accounting, finally—although the leader in a position of authority has access to the power that coerces, he makes use of that power only sparingly. He gives up little and gains much in employing self-restraint in the exercise of his power. For once he has gained the respect of associates, it is they, rather than the leader directly, who work to ensure compliance among the rest of their peers. Leaders only deplete their authority by an excess of use, and that excess is not long coming when leaders, having lost the respect of their subordinates, anxiously try to impose their will. Group experiments in sociology have found that the more often group leaders use the coercive power granted them, the more apt are they to be displaced. The experiments confirm what has long been thought; at its most effective, leadership is sustained by *noblesse oblige*, the obligation for generosity of behavior by those enjoying rank and power. Force is an ultimate resource that maintains itself by being seldom employed.

In a word, what instills confidence between superior and subordinate is joint commitment: commitment to one another and to agreed-upon organizational goals. It is this mutual commitment which encourages even the leader who is temperamentally inclined to retain the reins of power in his own hands to delegate not only responsibility but also authority to his subordinates, which allows him to rely more on corporate consensus than on authoritarianism in the making of decisions, and which, in turn, motivates the subordinate to request (or through muted symbolism, to demand) the exercise of responsibility and power commensurate with his position rather than to suffer in silence the close-handed intransigence of the oligarchic leader.

This train of thought need not be pursued very far in order to identify what has been emerging as one of the major contradictions facing modern organizations, including, as a prime special case, business organizations. This contradiction is found in the tendencies working simultaneously toward democratic rule and the more traditional authoritarian rule. This is something far deeper and more fundamental than a matter of the relationship between two or more individuals or even groups of individuals. It not only affects the style of management, the relationship between organizational units, the definition and operation of management, but touches upon the very purpose of the organization itself.

In recent years, behavioral scientists—notably such organizational investigators and theorists as McGregor, Herzberg, Argyris, Likert, Lawrence, and, in his own way, Peter Drucker—have shown to a growing number of corporate executives that efficiency and productivity lie in the direction of a more democratic or participative management. This proposition can be overstated and it often has been. Nevertheless, there is now a growing abundance of evidence testifying that *under certain conditions* democratic leadership is the more efficient in making for productivity of products *and* of valued human by-products.

All the same, styles of leadership continue to vary.

The repertoire of styles is extensive; and, it would seem, only few leaders have or acquire the versatility to shift from one to another style as changing circumstances require. There is the authoritarian style in which the leader is insistent, dominating, and apparently self-assured. With or without intent, he creates fear and then meets the regressive needs of his subordinates generated by that fear. He keeps himself firmly at the center of attention and manages to keep communication among the others in the system to a minimum. Ready to use coercion at the slightest intimation of divergence from his definitions of the situation, the authoritarian may be effective for a while in times of crisis when the organizational system is in a state of disarray. But, particularly for organizations in a democratically toned society, extreme and enforced dependence upon the leader means that the organizational system is especially liable to instability.

The democratic style of leadership, in contrast, is more responsive. It provides for extended participation of others, with policies more often emerging out of interaction between leader and led. It provides for the care and feeding of the self-esteem of members of the system, but not in that counterfeit style of spreading lavish flattery on all and sundry egos in the vicinity, after the fashion once advocated by the merchants of interpersonal relations who would have us make pseudo-friends by inauthentic expressions of sentimentality. (Remember G. K. Chesterton's finely wrought distinction: "Sentiment is jam on your bread; sentimentality, jam all over your face.") The democratic style of leadership does not call for indiscriminate and unyielding faith in your fellow man; some people are *not* to be trusted or respected or supported in their incompetence and willful malevolence. What the democratic style does call for is the introduction and maintenance of systems of relations which make for a grounded trust in others and for the human by-product of enabling people in the system to actualize their capacities for effective and responsible action and so to experience both authentic social relations and personal growth, each giving support to the other.

Precisely because one is committed to the ideal of democracy, one must be mindful of countertendencies in organizational systems. To begin with, there is a tendency toward what the German sociologist, Robert Michels, as long ago as 1915, excessively described as "the iron law of oligarchy." He was led to this "law" through which new organized minorities acquire dominion within organizations by examining the case of democratic organization. He found there the seeming paradox that leaders initially committed to democratic values abandoned those values as their attention turned increasingly to maintaining the organization and especially their own place within it. The danger is plain. Leaders long established are often the last to perceive their own transition toward oligarchy, toward a form of control in which power is increasingly confined to the successively few. And leaders long established are apt to confuse the legitimacy of their rule with themselves. We all remember that royal proclamation by Louis XIV: "L'état, c'est moi!" And we can recall the more recent story of de Gaulle periodically intoning to himself: "Quand je veux savoir ce que pense la France, je m'interroge" ("When I want to know what France thinks, I ask myself"). In this specific sense, many a long-established business leader is incorrigibly Gaullist.

The Michels brand of organizational pessimism poses grave problems for the business leader who would be both competitive and compassionate. The temper of the age suggests, however, the necessity of developing a response that utilizes a countervailing force to Michels' iron law. Such a force finds expression in the rule of thumb which says that the solution to the deficiencies of democracy is more democracy.

A particular ailment of organizational leadership was long since diagnosed by Chester Barnard as "the dilemma of the time lag." In this phrase he referred to the problem of discrepancy between organizational requirements for immediate adaptive action and the slow process of obtaining democratic approval of it. This is an authentic dilemma, not easily resolved. Democratically organized groups can cope with it only by having their members come to recognize *in advance* that, remote as they are from the firing line of daily decision, there will be occasions in which decisive action must be taken before it can be fully explored and validated by the membership. This comes hard for democratic organizations whose members often prefer to pay the price of recurrent maladaptations in order to avoid having their leadership converted into Caesarism or Bonapartism. But to earn the right for leases of independent decision, democratic leaders must provide for continuing accountability. They must be accountable not only in terms of the criteria they themselves propose but in terms of the often more extensive criteria adopted by other members of their organization and by the wider society.

This brings us straight to another ambivalence and dilemma confronting the organizational leader. One of the traditional responsibilities of the corporate leader, no less than the political one, and the cause of many contradictions in which the corporate executive is involved, is the need to balance the interests of groups which have a legitimate (and sometimes not so apparently legitimate) call on the resources of the organization.

The most obvious interest in the business corporation is economic and the most obvious interest groups are composed of employees, owners, and consumers. Striking a balance among these three groups alone—to say nothing here about the needs of increased capitalization, of the local community, and of the society beyond— poses basic contradictions of thought and action. In the one sphere of employee interests, for example, the business leader is often torn by the question of whether he should seek to attract labor at minimum cost or whether he should ensure for the organization a pool of quality labor by paying top dollar; whether he should place more or less emphasis on fringe benefits as opposed to wages and salaries; whether he should ensure security of employment to the possible short-term detriment of the corporation or whether he should seek maximum efficiency (which means, to put it bluntly, staff layoffs during periods of lax activity) to the possible long-term detriment of the corporation. Such questions are not completely resolved in the marketplace. The decisions turn more nearly on the system of values within which the corporation functions. These values, in turn, are imposed not so much by the economic function of the corporation as by its culture, traditions, history of recent experience, and by the personal proclivities of its leaders within the current context of the polity, the economy, and the society.

In this same sphere of employee interests, but now in a wider sense, the corporate leader must balance or arbitrate a secondary and often equally important interest: What is to be the share of the corporate resources allocated to each unit? What percentage of the budget will be allotted to manufacturing, research and development, advertising, computerization, the development of staff, and so on? It is a tempting belief that such questions are resolved in the organizational hierarchy solely by considerations of corporate need based on objective analysis and authoritative projections. But this is seldom the case. The business leader is as much circumscribed as the political leader by "political" constraints internal to the organization. And with all the accounting systems of planning, programming, and budgeting now in force and yet to come, one suspects that this will continue.

All this takes us back to the structural and functional aspects of the position of organizational leader. He is, of course and above all else, a maker of decisions; not, be it noted, *the* decision-maker. He differs from all the other makers of decision in the organization he leads in this: His decisions are ordinarily more consequential for the fate of that organization and for those parts of its environment affected by the ramified results of those decisions. He faces with fearsome regularity the need to assess conflicting interests, conflicting sentiments, and conflicting convictions within the organization. In this regard, there can be no rest for the sometimes weary leader. He is structurally located at the very node of conflicting wants and demands within the organization. His role requires him to acknowledge and work on these conflicts, not to deny them or to cover them over with the rhetoric of feigned consensus. He has the task of alerting the others to the sources of the conflict, to define and redefine the situation for them, to have them acknowledge in turn that decisions gauged in the light of the organization as a whole must often override the particular concerns of its parts.

It is no easy matter to discover what is in the best interest of the total organization, and so there is ample leeway for continuing disagreement. A degree of indeterminacy requires the exercise of reasonably confident judgment rather than the demonstration of certain outcomes. The leader may err in his calculated decisions engaging the conflicting interests and beliefs of his constituency. That is bad enough. But his greatest error comes in trying to evade these conflicts. Nothing catches up with an organizational leader so much as a conscientious policy of evasion which seeks the appearance of peace and quiet by avoiding decisions that might alienate this or that sector of the constituency. And *because* of a degree of indeterminacy about the validity of the decision, it is not merely the substance of his decisions that is consequential for the organization but the mode through which he arrives at them and the mode in which he makes them known. Effective leaders arbitrate and mediate the inevitable conflicts within the organization in such fashion that most of the members involved in his decisions feel most of the time that justice has been done. It is the role of the leader to act for the whole while interpreting for the parts. And so it is that even a substantively mistaken decision—as the limiting case— taken in ways that win the respect of associates and presented in ways that enlist their however reluctant assent will be less damaging than decisions which are substantively sound at the time but which have little support in the organization because they are taken as arbitrary and inequitable. The reason for this is plain enough. Organizational decisions become transformed into organizational realities only to the extent that they engage the willing support of those who must translate them into day-by-day practice. Without such support, the *initially* sound decision has a way of becoming converted into a subsequently unsound one.

Just as the corporate leader must balance the interests of interest groups within his organization, so he is caught in the even more difficult dilemma of balancing the interests of interest groups outside his organization. The direct relationship between the portions of economic wealth distributed by the corporation to its various primary "publics" is reasonably well understood. Should dividends greatly increase, there will be less under static conditions for distribution to the workers in the form of wages and to consumers in the form of stable or lower prices. But conditions are not static; indeed, it is one of the important functions of the private sector to see to it—through innovation, cost control, new efficiencies—that they never become static.

As a business grows in its capacity to create economic wealth, two interrelated phenomena occur, both of which establish new contradictions with which the organizational leader must cope. One is the demands of the traditional interest groups (employees, owners, consumers) for the production of wealth which is not essentially economic, that is, social wealth. The other is the rise of new interest groups which make other demands on the organization's resources for both economic and social wealth. A few topical examples will bring each of these developments to mind.

The rise of consumerism can be ascribed, at least in part, to a growing public which, surfeited with material possessions, now demands that these same possessions be imbued with qualities which are not only economically profitable but socially desirable. Thus, in our autos we demand seat belts rather than chrome strips; in our drugs, efficacy rather than palliatives (or worse); in our health care, adequacy for all rather than for the few. In like fashion, the call for "relevance" and "meaning" in work cannot be ascribed only to the altogether alienated few but must be recognized as also representing the deepest drives for self-actualization and self-esteem among those who, already employed, have found a measure of economic security. Finally, we can discern the faint beginnings of social commitment among at least a few of the twenty-eight million stockholders in this country—the clearest example being the voting of church-owned stock in an effort to achieve, in particular companies, the employment and advancement of minorities.

The second phenomenon is a corollary of business success. That success attracts notice and consequently increased demands, of both an economic and social kind. Thus, eleemosynary associations find their way to the corporate doorstep seeking contributions; quasi-public associations of all kinds place demands on the corporation which are not only financial but managerial (the time of staff) and physical (meeting sites); and on occasion entire communities descend on the successful corporation to seek aid in cleaning up the air and water (which, be it noted, the corporation has often helped to pollute), in employing the unemployed, in creating needed public transportation.

But if success brings enlarged demands, it also brings enlarged obligations for the corporation to engage in public service. The corporation, particularly the large and successful one, cannot stand aloof from the society in which it exists, if for no other reason—and there are other reasons—than its own economic health. In the last analysis, in this democratic republic at least, every corporation exists at the suffrance of society. To continue to exist, the corporation must meet its obligations, and not particularly those which it accepts as its own but those which are placed on it by society.

Thus, the leader of a significant business corporation must be both a "local" and a "cosmopolitan." By a local, I mean one who is largely oriented to his organization or immediate community which dominates his interests, concerns, and values. By a cosmopolitan, I mean one who is oriented toward the larger social world beyond his immediate organization or community, with extended interests, concerns, and values. The effective leader of a major business faces the task of combining both orientations and developing capabilities appropriate for putting both into practice. He must be able to look inward at his organization and outward at its concentric zones of environment. Social change has reduced his realistic options. Now, more than ever before, he must be both local and cosmopolitan. For although organizations have always been part of a larger social system and an ecosystem, the extent and character of those linkages were for a long time not widely noticed. With the spread of education—defective as it often is—all this is changing. Awareness of the interrelations involved in the ecosystem and social system is developing in every sector of our society. For leaders of business the enlarged awareness means that they must abandon the spectacular malapropism of not so long ago: "What's good for business is good for society." They must transform it into the countermaxim: "What's good for society is good for business—even when it's seemingly not."

In short, the leaders of business in the morally more sensitive society of our time are coming to recognize that they must pay the price of a growing commitment to the moral purposes of the larger society. Acting in terms of an authentic moral commitment is not cost-free. It comes at a price, a price paid for what that society has been contributing and continues to contribute to its constituent organizations. For, as the economists tell us in their analyses of "market externalities," the price system often fails to account for the benefits received or the costs suffered by those who are not directly parties to a transaction. The beneficiaries of technological change, for example, are at best only a small part of those who suffer from their deleterious secondary consequences (as the report on the assessment of technology by the National Academy of Sciences reminds us) and as we observe for ourselves while suffering our polluted environments of air, water, sound, landscape, and society.

Conceding that the private sector of our economy does have a role in helping to solve public problems, regardless of whether its role is in competition or in cooperation with government, it is evident that the traditional concepts of competition, within and among companies, are being redefined in confronting those problems. One reason is that the problems themselves are so immense that their solution will require all of the organizations' competitive energies; another is that the face of the competitive "enemy" has changed: It is the problem itself, rather than, in the first instance, another company or another industry. These competitions continue, of course, but they are caught up in larger purposes. This notion finds analogy in the American mission-to-the-moon project, which was not a triumph of competition alone (if we put aside the jingoistic impetus to the program: "Beat Russia"). It was a triumph of cooperation. Within that, it was a triumph of managerial ability in getting thousands of organizations and millions of individuals to collaborate in the attainment of one overarching goal. Actually, the contradictions apparent in this example are socially generated rather than inevitably imposed. For as behavioral studies have shown—and as every business leader knows from experience in his own organization—the fruits of cooperation are far more abundant than those of competition. The basic contradictions, then, may lie within our institutions, within our social and cultural patterns, and derivatively in our assumed psychologcal needs and aspirations.

Finally, in raising questions about the very purpose of our business organizations, we find basic ambivalences which must at one time or another plague every corporate executive: Does the successful business try first to profit or to serve? The quick, agile answer—it tries to do both—escapes the dilemma by swift flight from it. Leaders of business have only begun to wrestle with the problem of *how* to do both in appropriate scale. For they are at work in a rapidly changing moral environment which requires them to make new assessments of purpose. This is a tough assignment. I have alluded to the increasing moral sensibility of American society, knowing that I cannot actually demonstrate that increase beyond all reasonable doubt, let alone measure its extent. All the same, it seems to me that evidence for it abounds on every side. Most of all, it is found in our national inventory of self-critical diagnoses. In growing numbers, we Americans direct our critical attention to the shortcomings of our society just as we have long directed our admiring attention to its strengths. The more we demand of our society, the more the faults we find in this process of collective self-scrutiny. As we raise our sights and enlarge our moral expectations, we become more sensitive to the inequities of our society, its corruptions, and its unrealized potentials for a humane life. Unlike an apathetic society, or a complacent one, a self-critical society represents a heightened moral sensibility. What was good enough before, in the form of convenient compromises with moral principle, is no longer judged good enough. More and more Americans are stirring themselves out of the complacency induced by affluence to ask the harder questions: affluence for what? and for whom? and what beyond affluence?

Leaders of organizations in this changing moral environment are being pressed to become agents for the enlarging of equity and humane life. The range of their options is becoming delimited. For should they choose to believe that *only* the fiscal record of profit can testify to the success of their organizations, they will find this self-defeating. In due course, they will find that even that restricted index of accomplishment will deteriorate as they remain on the periphery of the great social transformations of our time. With a degree of optimism, one can be persuaded that newly emerging orientations in the private sector of the nation's business, with their attendant contradictions, ambiguities, and doubts, will force a fresh examination of the social role of business and of the business leader, and that this examination will result in an extended, viable place for the ideal of social commitment in this revolutionary society.

And still the question remains: How shall the leaders of organizations steer their course through the ambivalences and contradictions of leadership? What concepts shall they use as their guide? Written by a man who has known throughout his adult life the pleasures and pains of leadership, the speeches in this book may be instructive.

Part 1
The Individual

"The Responsibilities of Leadership" is, at one level, a simple declaration of faith; at a deeper level, however, it is a summation of the fundamental truths which experience has taught. For Mr. Oates is concerned not with tenets but with feelings: "Sensitivity to your fellow human beings is primary"; not with past accomplishments but with future opportunities: "Progress is attained only when high aspirations have become possibilities and men have gone out to seize them"; not with glory but humility: The leader "must find his support for continued leadership from below."

The next two speeches expand this theme. In "Change—Renewal—Imagination," Mr. Oates asks for "the assimilation of new goals, new routines, and new attitudes and new relationships," and above all he asks that this process be approached with "a consciousness of joy." To accomplish the objective of adapting to change and, indeed, of promoting change, he calls for "a built-in system of self-criticism" through which one may pursue a program of both personal and organizational renewal. Finally, he bids people, in all of their activities, to employ their imagination, for "it is only through imagination that men become aware of what the world might be."

"Information *Is Not Enough*" carries Mr. Oates' appeal for "feeling" relationships a step further. In it, he shuns a discussion of media and technique and talks instead of "helping people to understand each other better and to trust each other." Business organizations, suggests Mr. Oates, must give all people "an opportunity to grow to the limits of their respective abilities. And this means, among other things, that they must be given the information they solicit and think they need and not just what we think they need." With a telling bit of humor, he adds, "Skeletons can be taken out of closets and even rattled a little bit. . . . When you look a skeleton right in the face it is not very gruesome."

Such sentiments have led Mr. Oates inevitably into fields of voluntary service. In easier days—before the needs of the nation became so painfully obvious—he, like many of his business peers, was content to affirm the historical quality of cooperativeness and to urge his listeners to participate for the personal rewards inherent "*In the Service of Man.*" In later years, however, his tone has become more urgent and his corporate and private actions have presaged his tone. His own involvements have taken on a new relevance, his understanding has become deeper, and his call to the business community has become clearer and more insistent. He has asked: "Do I have a responsibility in all this?" His response has been immediate and unreserved: "We are literally faced with the task of saving a nation and its people— today!"—B.C.B.

The Responsibilities
of Leadership

We are confronted almost daily with a wide range of comment about "leadership." Some assert that only the selfish and venal succeed; that there exists no true equality of opportunity and that achievement is usually the consequence of influence or favoritism and not the reward of merit and effort.

Others claim to be discoverers of patent formulas guaranteed to produce high office in any field in ten easy lessons or with six short and insipid prayers. And still others discourage the pursuit of accomplishment in the affairs of man, urging that such success is unworthy and debasing.

Amid all this conflict and confusion we hear—more frequently the older we grow—the inner voice calling us back to simple, timeless verities and basic articles of faith.

This has been a continuing theme since 1958 in speeches delivered before diverse audiences of students, businessmen, churchmen, and civic activists.

We must, it seems to me, recognize initially that "the maintenance of leadership is a restless occupation." You cannot just learn what leadership involves, memorize it, and say, "That is that." You will remember that Justice Holmes has told us: "Certainty is an illusion and repose is not the destiny of man."

Just what is this evasive thing we call leadership? We have all heard many speeches on the subject and we have read books on it. We know that it involves attitudes, ideals, and techniques, and we know that it has its rewards and its heavy responsibilities. It is a lonely position. There is no loneliness to equal that of the man who has to make the final decision.

Someone has said that leadership is the art of inducing someone else to do your work better than you could do it yourself. This somewhat glib observation refers, I take it, to administrative or executive leadership. Professional leadership is different. A member of a profession becomes a leader, not in the sense of being a supervisor or boss, but in the sense of becoming preeminent in a defined field of intellectual activity primarily dedicated to public service.

But whatever may be the nature of our work or the character of our own vocational activity, eminence always involves the following:

1. The determination to excel.
2. The willingness to pay the price, to study, to live through disappointments with optimism—to accept the sacrifices necessary to succeed.
3. The steadfast pursuit of purpose, doing the work

day after day, week after week—yes, year after year—whether you feel like doing it or not.

4. And finally, pride and faith in the virtue of your calling; that is to say, spiritual motivation.

These are the basic factors of success, as I see them.

And then, having reached a position of leadership, you are, to your horror and amazement, an example. You may not want to face it, but it is an inevitable and implicit fact. You cannot let others be disappointed in your conduct or beliefs. If a leader lets his associates down, he betrays not only those people looking to him as an example, but he also betrays success itself. For if the leader is unworthy, who wants to emulate his success? Why try to succeed? As a leader you are no longer free to do as you please in large areas of your life. Actually, you are limited by the necessity of relentless discipline. And, oh, how often you fail to exercise that discipline.

As a leader you must first fight for humility. There is, fortunately, a helpful guide in this fight—the knowledge that no one is indispensable and that everyone must find his support for continued leadership from below. You just cannot succeed without the support of your associates and subordinates. You are just as good as they know you to be.

You must have another talent—that of winning success every day: "Leadership *is* a restless occupation." Government leaders must meet the challenge of the ballot box each two, four, or six years. Indeed, all of us must stand for reelection each day—reelection expressed in terms of daily tasks successfully accomplished in collaboration with our fellow human beings; accomplishments representing new votes of confidence in our reliability, integrity, and acumen. To get "reelected" you must seek ceaselessly to attain the highest possible standards of belief and deportment.

Striving for the highest standards of business morality means trying to be right, not just legal. I believe that there is a natural law—that all men at all times must seek righteousness and that it is always wrong to lie, steal, or injure others. It is just not so that the only guide to right or wrong is the last decision of the Supreme Court. Doing what is right sometimes takes high courage—moral courage to live up to our convictions, resist gnawing temptations, overcome weakness, perform unpopular or disagreeable tasks, take responsibility, and accept the consequences of our acts.

Man achieves success because he has nobility in his heart and aspiration in his soul. In our heart of hearts we know there is such a thing as righteousness. If you are sincere in your determination to seek nobility and righteousness, you must serve certain ideals and possess certain qualities.

Moral courage is one such quality. Courage has the same basic character whether the circumstances present an incidental and inconspicuous human problem or an imperative national or world-wide issue such as the one Winston Churchill faced in rallying Britain when, in 1940, it stood alone in defense of human freedom. It is not, therefore, either fatuous or unrealistic to remember what Churchill said.

After the disaster in Norway and with the Germans streaming into France, Churchill became Prime Minister and his first words in Parliament were: "I have nothing to offer but blood, toil, tears and sweat. You ask what is our aim? I can answer in one word—Victory. Victory at all costs. Victory in spite of all terror. Victory however long and hard the road may be."

And three weeks later came Dunkirk—300,000 men saved but their equipment all left in France, and Churchill growled: "We shall not flag or fail. We shall go on to the end. We shall never surrender."

And when Paris and France fell and General Weygand said, "The English will have their necks wrung in three weeks," Churchill replied, "The battle of France is over. The battle of Britain is about to begin. Upon it depends our way of life. Let us therefore brace ourselves to our duties and so bear ourselves that if the British Empire and its Commonwealth last for a thousand years, men will still say this was their finest hour."

There are additional qualities of leadership which are most likely to stand you in good stead and to contribute to your individual success.

The first such quality is sensitivity. At the very heart of our national ideal stands the noble and spiritual belief in the dignity and sanctity of the individual human being. This means that not only do we need response from others, but we need the capacity in ourselves to respond naturally and intimately to others. We simply can't go it alone. We learn to be responsive by concerning ourselves with others, not persuading others to be concerned with us. We know that the world is in

33

desperate need of solutions to its problems, but we know intuitively that it needs kindness more. Sensitivity to your fellow human beings at all levels, then, is a primary quality of leadership.

The next quality involves an appreciation of and respect for honor. It is widely recognized that one basic element which all humans hold in common is the desire for recognition. I suspect that the highest, and perhaps the only pure, form of recognition is to be known as an honorable man. This is a quality which is unmistakably valid and universally cherished. But one must earn the right to be recognized as an honorable man. One must meet the standards of honor. People are not honored for what they have given. You will remember the timeless phrase of Henry V on the field of Agincourt, "If it be a sin to covet honor, I am the most offending soul alive."

Nothing has a higher rank in human attainments than the possession of a quiet sense of security. Only when that sense is possessed does a reassuring comfort arise which releases the energy required to meet the unknown future with confidence. This confidence will always come to the man who, with humility, selects a high and noble goal and pursues it with full and sacrificial effort and a pure conscience. The world instantly recognizes and accepts such men as its leaders. Whatever the goal you seek, be sure that it is so designed as to bring out the best of which you are capable. If you do this, you have succeeded—whatever may be your status or your calling.

And finally, there is that great experience life provides: adventure. All leaders know that they must risk greatly to experience great rewards. No age in history has more clearly called for responsible innovation (which means risk) and confident courage than our own. Indeed, throughout human history, progress is attained only when high aspirations have become possibilities and men have gone out to seize them.

And so, may I implore you to nourish your sensitivity to human needs and your capacity to respond; to hold close and guard jealously your respect for honor; to carve out for yourselves, and for others, secure places in the larger scheme of things; and to embrace adventure and change with courage and confidence, always remembering that not to change can also be leadership.

Change–Renewal–
Imagination

It is said we are Adam on the threshold of a new world. The man born in the Stone Age died in the Stone Age; but we have been through so many "ages" even in our own lives that our age can't be given a name except the "Age of Change." We pray that man will have sufficient maturity to make it the "Age of Human Progress" and not simply "Change."

Yet perhaps, after all, the two are synonymous. The longer I live the more vivid and real becomes one important truth: Progress springs from tensions. This truth, I think, is pointed up well in an epigraph written by Caryl B. Haskins:

> The great ages of mankind, the ages of the most radical changes and the longest advances, the ages

Compiled from three speeches on these subjects given between 1960 and 1969 before business and university groups.

that later generations of men called great, were not the times of easy optimism when men thought everything was discovered, everything architectured, everything finished. Greatness and ease, vast innovative and untroubled stability are no more compatible among nations or in a world community than they are among individuals.

One of our most valuable human instincts (and thank God we've got it!) is to get on top of our job, to know it, to understand it, to breathe it, sleep it, and perfect our performance in it. Every man has the dream that some day there will be no unanswered questions; there will be no papers on the desk; the job will run itself because he has mastered it.

Well, of course, that's a dream. It isn't life. Such an operation we regard as a job on the tracks. But there is implicit in such a situation a fear of change, a refusal to innovate, a vigorous resistance to a newcomer or a new thought that might disturb our satisfaction, our peace of mind, the even tenor of our ways. The first thing you know, when you get the job on the track, is that you've got yourself in a rut and you don't want anybody to make any suggestions. "Get away from me, get away! I've done this for forty years and this is the way it's done. We know."

Certainly in this age the very essence of the administrative job is the administration of change, and this is no mean task. Adaptation to change involves the assimilation of new goals, new routines, and, toughest of all, new attitudes and new relationships. It means the abandonment of existing and accepted objectives and relations—those very forces which have kept the organization together.

We must learn to meet the challenge in this, our changing age, with all assurance of triumph and with a consciousness of joy in the process. Some, of course, will ask why we must change. There are two answers. First, because life is changing all around us. We are forced to change in order to breathe the very air in which we live. And second, because we can and should do a better job. We are required to improve in order to meet the competitive challenges of the hour and the needs of the American people for the services we are called upon to provide.

Actually, you know, change is a necessary fact of creative life, of continuing life, and the only possible basis for improvement of opportunity. I suppose opportunity is always the companion of self-renewal. Unless you and I individually and conscientiously take steps to be reborn, to renew ourselves, we will become stagnant, and in terms of creativity we will expire. Change is always in the air, everywhere, which means that opportunity is always in the air, everywhere. The rewards of the future will belong to those who accept innovation and embrace sound change and recognize it as the companion of opportunity.

I suggest, therefore, that it is highly relevant to analyze what is involved in self-renewal. No management can face the future with all of its complexities without a conscious search for the quality of self-renewal.

We must develop an effective self-discipline, a process of self-improvement and self-development. Now, what are a few concepts that may help?

First, I would respectfully suggest that we must have a built-in system of self-criticism, one which allows the criticism to be communicated up as well as down. Now, it takes an awful lot of candor and frankness and mutual trust to engage in criticism up as well as down. It's hard to expect a subordinate to be brutally frank with the boss. But we must learn to accept a suggestion from an associate or a subordinate as a help and not as bad news or discouragement. I know, and I know very well indeed, that top management cannot always furnish itself adequate self-criticism. It needs it coming from below very, very much.

Second is the concept of flexibility, the spirit of flexibility, particularly in regard to jurisdictional boundaries, personal empires if you please, rules and procedures. Many a rule book is filled with rules written to solve problems that no longer exist. The book gets thicker, the ideas thinner. Jurisdictional lines tend to become sanctified. But I respectfully suggest that important and fundamental changes are wholesome, because they crack the cement, remove the odor of sanctification, and release the spirit for a new and enlightened opportunity.

Self-renewal is also dependent upon thinking about the future, not the past or the present. Of course, we've got to think about the present hard enough to get through it into the future. But we should never engage in nostalgia unless we are quite confident that the past— all of it, good, bad, and indifferent—will not come back.

Number four, the spirit and morale of the entire organization has to be conducive to, and accept the basic importance of, self-renewal. The spirit and morale of the organization must be such as to create in each person an acceptance, way down deep, that everyone's best interest and greatest opportunities depend upon the vitality of a self-renewing institution. May I respectfully say, therefore, that we should address ourselves to the task of re-creating ourselves individually, and together re-creating our whole business enterprise, constantly and forever.

It has frequently occurred to me that a final essential ingredient for self-renewal is the quality of imagination. It has been said that "man consists of body, mind and imagination." His body is faulty, his mind untrustworthy, but his imagination has made him remarkable. Indeed, it is only through imagination that men become aware of what the world might be.

There are many functions of imagination and, therefore, a number of different tasks for it to perform. Imagination permits what exists to be improved. It conceives, captures, and reproduces the beauty and glory of the fine arts. The great achievements of imagination are revealed through the ages by the brilliant prediction of new truths which seem to be impossible. These past prophets dreamt dreams, big dreams, and in a big way.

But the world and its progress, I submit, are dependent upon the continuing daily performances of the imaginations of thousands of men and women. Indeed, in every life and every age there is need for continuous creative thought to assure survival. Your imagination must develop feasible plans to permit adjustment to constantly changing environments. Indeed, your success in life will depend at all times and everywhere on the effectiveness and nobility of your imagination. Your position in life will reflect and respond to your dreams. Your individual futures will be the measure of your dreams and your imagination—nothing more, nothing less.

There are, however, certain guideposts which can help one to discover good and noble dreams. The first one is that all dreams, all imaginative plans must be consistent with knowledge. In this regard, may I call your attention to a basic and universal rule, namely, that all knowledge, in its entirety, on all subjects, constitutes a great single unit. Every dream must be disciplined and feasible and consistent with that which has heretofore been discovered and proved to be true. The fundamental reason why the astronauts could make their successful journeys in space is that the scientific laws heretofore discovered could be relied upon to operate everywhere.

In the next place, your dreams must be responsible and not simply emotional or personally appealing. It has been said that imagination is something which the world both calls for and fears. Its lack is a limitation on life, and its threat of unbalance a danger. Between these two extremes—the lack of imagination and imagination which is unstable emotionalism—lies the possibility of the development of this most vital power into a disciplined and mature faculty, into an instrument of broad insight and understanding.

The third and final guidepost for your dreams is that you must make sure that they are designed always to further the dignity, welfare, and sanctity of the individual man.

These are the three guideposts, then: Dreams must be

consistent with truth, responsible, and nobly motivated in terms of service.

Let me suggest that if we can accept and welcome the fact of change, if we seek daily to renew ourselves and our institutions, if we employ our imaginations for noble purposes, then we will be fulfilling our individual lives by giving the best that is in us.

Information

Is Not Enough

I have concluded that if there was anything that I had learned during my experience practicing law, in business, at work and play, and in curricular and extracurricular activities, it is that information alone isn't enough to achieve effective and workable communication between human beings.

What is required, above all, is the creation and maintenance of personal relationships that permit the free and accurate two-way transmission of information, that promote mutual confidence and respect, and that strengthen all participants in their capacity to perform their common tasks.

There exists a very demonstrable and highly unfortunate gap between our understanding of, and our technical achievements in, this field of communication and our

Excerpted principally from a speech delivered in 1961 before the Southern Gas Association meeting in New Orleans.

actual accomplishments. One of the most exasperating areas which illustrates the size of that gap involves the effort to persuade a substantial business organization to control costs. I don't know of anything more important than to develop with managerial personnel a sincere desire to attain efficient and prudent results through the method of cost control. Yet the response we frequently receive in reply to the call to control costs as compared with the action we need is most disconcerting.

Now I submit that this gap cannot be closed by more information—just more facts. No, information is probably already adequate in quantity and in quality, but information is not enough. I suggest that the method of imparting information and basing a call for action thereon is probably more important than the facts imparted and the eloquence of the call.

It occurs to me that information must be so presented as to gain certain intangible results such as pride, confidence, satisfaction, trust, and a desire to do something. Without these elements, mere facts are sterile, unproductive, and even antagonistic—at best they fall on deaf ears.

My experience indicates that generally a good communication atmosphere should be characterized by two basic conditions. Number one, people should have an opportunity to hear about what they are interested in and to receive information they need and want, from whom they want. And second, that the information be so presented as to produce absolute confidence in its authenticity and credibility and under circumstances and conditions which permit communication up and down.

Now, this is in addition to the traditional activities in this field. We, of course, still need and must rely upon on-the-job instruction as well as upon our formal communication programs—bulletins, periodicals, hand books, suggestion systems, meetings, dinners, service anniversaries, and all the other methods used to announce policies and programs. I believe that a pretty good job is generally being done throughout industry on these formal programs. But the formal programs still leave the communication gap.

There are basic factors in our business environment today which tend to raise bars to effective communication. The increasing growth in the size of our organizations—growth in volume, growth in complexity and perplexity—has resulted in an ever-increasing need to specialize. And when you specialize you create narrow management. You run the risk of having your specialists more interested in their respective professions (perhaps more interested in their professional associations) than in the institution which employs them and with which they have cast their lot.

Similarly, the dream of every business official is to have the job so set up and so operating that it runs itself. There is no such thing. But that we must try to achieve it is, it seems to me, very important. Yet this instinct reduces the willingness and capacity of business administrators to embrace innovation, and is one of the real obstacles to effective communication. Nobody wants the newcomer, the new idea, the boat-rocker. And that attitude, seen ever so many times, results in suspicion, jealousy, false pride, and a sense of either desertion or isolation. The private domain concept does not promote understanding. It does prevent coordination and militates against teamwork.

Now, the instinct is to combat these environmental factors of "specialization" and of "private domain" by imparting more and more information, by making more and more studies, and by preparing more and more graphs. But because of the very character of the factors which create the climate, I submit that the mere transmission of information isn't the answer.

The tasks which these factors necessarily present include such intangibles as helping people to understand each other better and to trust each other. You need to increase pride and confidence in all fellow workers and in the company as a whole. May I respectfully suggest that we in American business today must accept the necessity of providing an opportunity for the exercise of initiative by our employees in obtaining information of interest to them and under circumstances that allow for varying individual interests, doubts, and curiosities.

I will briefly give you an illustration of this proposal. In our management development program we recruit as the faculty the top officers of the company. It is their task to present information—about our objectives, our goals, our basic policies—to throw out problems, express opinions, and make suggestions. We solicit comments and criticisms and then we field the questions.

It is amazing to watch the suspicions creep away, the faces clear, and the doubts vanish. Skeletons *can* be taken out of closets and even rattled a little bit. You know, when you look a skeleton right in the face it is not very gruesome. Soon a warmth, a joint interest, and a sense of mutual concern permeate the meeting as we together realize the magnitude and difficulty of the problems we face and as we realize that everyone has problems, frequently the same problems, and that there is no royal road to success. The top officers suddenly become people, fellow human beings with problems, worries, dreams, and ideals.

They recognize that there are areas, of course, where you cannot answer a question, either because you do not know the answer or because the question is premature or because the rights and interests of others preclude discussion. But when you give the reason why you can't discuss it, everyone is completely satisfied.

Now, we have primarily made it plain that information is not limited to on-the-job announcements or instructions or to what management unilaterally chooses to release in formal programs to everybody. Our people have been given an opportunity to obtain the information they feel they need. Parenthetically, it is emphasized that it is their duty to pass on the information they get to their own groups. They have also had a chance to voice opinions and suggestions and to experience a sincere and considerate hearing for their views. They even report that I seem to have gotten something out of the meeting—*and indeed I have.*

This program is, of course, not new and not unique, but it deserves analysis because such analysis reveals certain basic truths about communication to which it is desirable frequently to return.

A faculty from the outside could teach management

principles and philosophy probably much more skillfully than we do; but the confidence, satisfaction, pride, and loyalty of the participants are produced by the interaction both between themselves and with the senior managers.

The Equitable is rather a large institution and many of the people are strangers to each other. People constituting a cross section of middle management who have known each other for twenty or thirty years only as names on an organization chart or as telephone extension numbers suddenly meet each other as human beings and exchange views.

These men say: "Now I know someone over there personally. Now I know that he has problems." Top management (the faculty) has developed in willingness to give and to give freely—and I certainly include myself in this development.

These experiences, I am sure, have bolstered the dependability, validity, and reputation of our other more formal communication programs. There are, of course, dangers. The majority of top management must accept and support these ideas wholeheartedly or else the whole thing will fall on its face. The intangibles we have been talking about depend absolutely on the accuracy, reliability, and effectiveness of the material we present and the painstaking care of our preparation. This is and must be no hit-or-miss performance. Such an approach would be fatal.

As we deal honestly and trustfully with our internal organization, so too do we attempt to deal with our external publics. A good public image for a company cannot be fabricated out of clever publicity. Like all progressive companies, we are increasingly concerned with the problem of shaping effective and active roles for ourselves—not mere images. This, it seems to me, is the only sure way to long-term success.

Within the Equitable, therefore, our conception and implementation of public relations are guided by such considerations. As a company, we take quite seriously the three main conclusions of a book entitled *The Corporation and Its Publics*, which was edited by one of our own officers, Dr. John W. Riley, Jr.:

That public relations must play a key role in deciding and executing those actions of the corporation most appropriate to the "public interest."

That public relations people must be increasingly well trained in the substantive disciplines—particularly in the behavioral sciences.

That effective public relations programs will be increasingly based on continuous research with the many publics that ultimately will join in granting social survival to the corporation.

It is a working principle with us that society itself is essentially a system of interdependent parts, that a change in one part cannot occur without creating changes in others. If one area is economically depressed, or enlightened by a new sense of participation, or burdened by crime and delinquency, or lifted by vision and imagination, or blighted by monopolistic power—then it surely follows that other parts of society will feel the same consequences.

We also need periodically to remind ourselves that any

type of enterprise, system, or organization must be constantly renewed if it is to survive. We must strive for the wisdom, adaptability, and inspiration required to meet the demands of self-renewal.

Finally, it is believed that an essential responsibility of any business enterprise is to conduct its affairs in such a way as to maintain and enhance the worth of the individual human being. Certainly the individual on the job is now regarded not as an economic man who works merely for economic ends, but as an individual with values and emotional involvements of his own. He has come to be recognized as a person seeking a personal and social identity, as one who must have a view of himself not simply as an anonymous contributor to some larger whole but as a person with his own unique integrity and sanctity. No longer does responsible management widely believe that human beings have an inherent dislike for work. We now know that a man's potential is far from circumscribed and that it is our responsibility to see to it that every individual, irrespective of creed or background, has equal opportunity for maximum development.

All people must be given an opportunity to grow to the limits of their respective abilities. And this means, among other things, that they must be given the information they solicit and think they need and not just what we think they need; and they must receive it in a way and under circumstances that will win their respect and confidence, namely, in a way that is convincing as to authenticity, integrity, and validity.

If we are to grow in this nation—if our businesses are

to grow and thereby live—we must tap the full potential of our people, increase productivity, overcome resistance to change, and make innovation feasible and welcome. To accomplish these aims, good communication is essential. We can't say: "Gentlemen, I wish I had time to give attention to these things." This *is* our lifeline!

In the Service
of Man

In his long and hard climb to civilization, man has miraculously emerged, characterized by an impulse to help his neighbor in the hour of need. In an earlier day, communities were established and sustained because of this common acceptance of personal responsibility.

We are now, of course, in the anomalous position of living in great metropolitan areas where your neighbor is a stranger. I don't suppose I know a fourth of my fellow tenants in the apartment house in which I live. I may know them to recognize their faces, but I don't know them by name—and they are my neighbors. I'm living closer to the man across the hall than any pioneer ever lived to his neighbor and I don't even know him on the street.

This has been a recurring theme in speeches before student and business audiences over the last decade.

Yet the innate willingness to accept a measure of personal responsibility for improving the state of society and alleviating human and social needs persists. We have formed a legion of philanthropic institutions and service organizations. We are furthermore encouraged by our national tax policy to engage, through private initiative, in good works. As Americans, we do share a responsibility to give of our time and our personal funds to specific causes.

But financial support and professional leadership of charitable organizations can never be adequate or meaningful substitutes for the compelling interest of individuals whose hearts respond to human needs. Individuals lose irrevocably if their only concern for welfare is (like taxes) remote, impersonal, and detached. It is a privilege and not a burden to accept the responsibilities of stewardship.

The last decade has seen a combination of awesome developments, punctuated by events of horrible as well as glorious potentials. Sputnik, Selma, assassinations, missiles, organ transplants, Vietnam, Berkeley and now Harvard, Biafra, the Middle East, Cuba, Czechoslovakia, the *Pueblo*, men on the moon. The good, the bad, the promising, the ominous, the inspiring—together a bewildering succession of happenings.

It seems incredible now to think back on the days when most of us chose the luxury of being simply observers from a back seat, picking those events out of the daily news which did not shock our well-protected sense of complacent well-being.

And if we stumbled into an unpleasant set of circumstances, or became exposed to bitter discrimination, agonizing poverty, or destructive decay, we were usually able to convince ourselves that such horrors concerned only the other fellow, and to tell ourselves that it could never happen to us.

My good friends—such a situation exists no more.

Is there anyone here today who has not been shocked by a picture of an urban disturbance, or a poverty-stricken family, or a student rebellion, and who has not asked himself at least once: Do I have a responsibility in all this?

Perhaps in this broad, complex land of ours there still remain many Americans who prefer to think comfortable vintage thoughts of "the good old days." We, however, have chosen not to be numbered among them. And there's not a moment to lose in the development of a truly formidable and effective attack on national decay of all kinds—moral as well as physical. There are time bombs ticking in our cities.

The future will reflect our reaction to the urgency of the present. We have always had problems in this country. Domestic tranquillity, although a basic constitutional objective, has not been our hallmark. Consider the harsh problems and the Indians of the frontier, the agonizing questions of states' rights, the bloody period of outright civil warfare, the seemingly endless struggles between labor and capital, and the economic convulsions which led to the search for monetary stability.

Time was a luxury we thought we could afford *then*. But the network of mass communications which today detail and widely scatter the ever-proliferating problems of our cities will not let us forget, even for a few moments, the desperate challenges and shining opportunities which are at hand *now*.

We should be proud of the fact that our own business has been among the leaders of American institutions in responding to this imperative need for involvement. A good example is its recent allocation of a second billion dollars for low-income housing and the creation and sustenance of job-creating enterprises for our disadvantaged neighbors.

I suppose that each of us from time to time has wondered if our business was becoming too involved. We ask ourselves: What are the consequences of individual commitment and action? Will we be unnecessarily and unprofitably diverted from our proper pursuits? Will we be overcome and absorbed by these great and complex problems?

Some of the answers to these questions are to be found in historical statistics. For example, ten years ago there were 110 million individual life insurance policyholders. Today, there are well over 130 million. Life insurance in force has doubled in ten years and today we are well over the trillion mark. Studies conducted by the Institute of Life Insurance respecting public attitudes tell us that more and more people recognize and agree that social involvement is a good and proper role for business.

It is very clear that our business has not been diverted from its primary and fundamental responsibilities.

But even if there were signs that our attempts to improve the quality of life for all Americans were diverting us from certain business goals, our social involvement would be no less imperative, no less needed than it is now. The stakes are just that high. We are literally faced with the task of saving a nation and its people—today!

To those of you who have sensed the need to participate but who have yet to find your special niche for voluntary service, I suggest Socrates' admonition: Know thyself. If we take Socrates seriously—as we must—it means painful self-reexamination within the context of these rapidly changing conditions in our country. We must ask ourselves some tough questions.

Are we truly concerned for *human* reasons by urban unrest and riot, by the squalor and poverty in which so many fellow human beings live, by the inability of our minorities to compete educationally and economically, or do we see today's problems only in cold economic terms which we are powerless as individuals to do anything about?

If our interest is real and active, if we have real compassion, I say the opportunities for rewarding service are boundless.

But how, you may ask, can one have assurance that the commitment of time and talent to a cause or organization will really be of help in solving critical problems? There is, in fact, a bewildering array of approaches to these problems and of organizations in which one can participate. We must learn to choose wisely, and as basic guidelines may I suggest that three criteria be applied in deciding which organizations or activities offer the best chance for individual action to further meaningful results.

Ask yourself, first, what is the organization's *reason* for being. Has it a real and specific objective? Is it to combat air or water pollution? Is it devoted to better housing, transportation, or schools? Does it mean to fight poverty and discrimination? Does it seek to improve the administration of criminal justice? Does it campaign for improved health service for all? If its reason for being has some such innate validity, I'd say it is a legitimate endeavor.

But should you find the goals of the organization somewhat less than pressing, if they are obscure or backward-looking or are simply clinging tightly to the *status quo*, you may be in the wrong ballpark.

Second, I would suggest that you examine the *realism* of the cause or service organization—realism as to what can be done and what cannot be done. It is not unusual to find an organization which sets its goals so high that defeat is virtually inevitable. By the same token, goals set too low are often not worth bothering about. Don't allow yourself to become involved in an organization which purports to know how to solve all of the problems, and don't bite off more than you can chew as an individual volunteer. And, ask yourself, does the organization have enough budget and staff, or a realistic chance of getting them, to carry out the work necessary to achieve its goals? Using realism in another context, ask yourself whether you have the abilities and skills as well as genuine interest which can really help the work of the organization. Most important, does the activity realistically involve in its basic planning and actual work some of the people whom it seeks to help?

And, third, how about *relevance?* Try to determine how the organization relates to the larger society within which it exists. Perhaps the best test here is to ask: Is the organization relevant in its relationships to the many segments of the area in which it operates?

If such a question seems abstract, it can easily be rephrased in terms of time and place. Is the organization timely? Is it wide of the temporal mark—too early or too late? Nor is the setting, the jurisdiction, or the physical site of an organization unrelated to our choice.

Reason, Realism, and Relevance—perhaps we might think of these as the three R's in our search for the most appropriate involvement.

In the last analysis, the very concept of individual freedom is at stake! It is hard for most Americans to realize that the survival of the very idea for which this nation stands is not inevitable. It will survive *only* if enough Americans care enough.

We need to become a society of citizens as strenuously concerned with the common good as Americans historically have been concerned with the individual good. Oliver Wendell Holmes, Jr., perhaps best established our collective mandate when he said: "As life is action and passion, it is required of a man that he should share the passion and action of his time, at the peril of being judged not to have lived."

Part 2

The Organization

In his first official speech, before one thousand long-service employees, Mr. Oates said, "Man possesses the sanctity of a human personality [which] no one—no society, no boss, indeed no government—can trample on. . . ." Within a few months he had developed a statement of nine "principles" which expressed that belief in terms of specific goals. "A Philosophy of Management" is a composite of those two speeches and a summation of the essential human character of Mr. Oates' stewardship.

It is with the same humanistic philosophy that Mr. Oates approaches the outside environment. *Private enterprise will succeed only to the extent that it serves the public welfare,* he says in "Private Management—A Public Trust." He adds a corollary: *To the extent that business does, in fact, succeed, its responsibility to serve the public welfare grows.* These thoughts provide a functional framework for business. For Mr. Oates they also provide the cornerstone of a corporate rationale which suggests the possibilities for human and organizational growth; his business "creed" outlines a way of proceeding.

In the remaining speeches, Mr. Oates deals with three of

the more salient facts facing business today: education, salesmanship, computerization.

"Business and the Liberal Mind" sets forth a simple yet fundamental belief: that the goals of private enterprise and liberal education are not antithetical at all, but are, in fact, identical. Each is concerned with the development of man. And toward that goal "there is no field of activity where human rights and values are better recognized and more sincerely served than in business management." Business and the liberally educated need each other, and the interaction between the two will enrich them both.

Most people, when they think of life insurance, think of salesmen, and often the image is uncomplimentary. But behind the image is a man or a woman, and it is this person who is the concern of Mr. Oates in "The Dignity of Selling." After a decade in the insurance business—and after countless talks before groups of insurance salesmen, sharing their hopes and fears, frustrations and exultations—Mr. Oates summed up what he had learned: "that no activity is more essential . . . than selling."

By 1962, Equitable had moved into the forefront of a new organizational environment in the insurance industry: that brought about by electronic data processing. With many business executives exclaiming as to the wonders of EDP and others warning of its consequences, Mr. Oates found it worthwhile to return to first values, to human values. In "Man, Organization, and the Computer," he speaks of the "problems of personnel, organization, environmental change." He is concerned with the possibilities of upgrading employees, with building cooperation among operating units, with learning precision of language, with eliminating drudge work, with enhancing research capabilities, with improving customer service, with the management of change. The years since, of course, have shown that he has focused on the correct questions.—B.C.B.

A Philosophy of
Management

Each businessman is required to develop a philosophy of business, and the starting place must be in his own concept of the nature of man. I believe that man is a being with dignity and that he possesses the sanctity of a human personality. He is, therefore, entitled to respect. No one—no society, no boss, indeed no government—can trample on the human personality with impunity. If man were an animal it would be efficient to treat him as an animal, to classify him, work him, fatigue him, depreciate him, discard him. But man is not an animal. He is a reasoning human being and, we are taught, made in the image of God.

It follows that each employee needs recognition, respect, and the sincere interest of his business supervisor.

Drawn from two speeches given before Equitable employees and managers in 1957 and 1958; adapted for a speech before the Chicago Bar Association in June, 1958.

He must have more than a passing opportunity to earn a livelihood; he must be provided with a reasonable framework for a life. A man needs more than food, shelter, and clothing; he needs an environment in which he can realize a substantial percentage of his dreams.

The job of effectively applying a business philosophy of this kind, other than by mere words, is a never-ending process. It helps sometimes to get down to fundamentals, and for that purpose I have worked out a few statements of principles—not because I think they are written in the stars forever, but because they will stimulate our thoughts together about this vital question of developing, maintaining, and continually improving relations with our employees.

This is not an easy problem and there is no sentimental solution. The understanding of people so that you can help them is not inconsistent with the proper disciplining of people. As a matter of fact, the foundation of your philosophy is an appreciation of the other fellow as a fellow human being with the same weaknesses and temptations, failures and successes, pains, prayers and tribulations that you and I have.

1. To recognize and respect the dignity and individuality of each employee and to treat him courteously and considerately, and to attract, select, place, and promote employees based on their qualifications for work requirements without discrimination.

This business philosophy is illustrated, I think, by the very familiar technique of the open door. Our doors must be open—if not literally, figuratively. I do not suppose there is any greater satisfaction in life than to have people come to you on the tough ones, whether they have any direct relation to the daily task or not. It is that type of an open door which epitomizes respect for human dignity.

2. To maintain fair and consistent standards of performance, objectively reflecting these standards in decisions concerning the promotion, compensation, and retention of each employee.

That is one of those things which is easy to say but another thing to do. To maintain fair and consistent standards of performance you first have to find out what they are. One of the most difficult jobs in a large organization is to have consistent standards; to find out what is a good day's work, what are the tests and measurements of performance. You need painstaking patience, to analyze what the jobs are, what their relationships are, what proper standards are. Therefore, I have asked for a study so that we can know the rudiments of performance.

This study is not intended to circumscribe or limit the operating freedom of action and authority of the line organization; exactly the contrary. It is to make it more flexible, to open it up, to give more freedom by indicating where the freedom is. We have all known that the most enchained people are those who do not know what the rules of the game are. It is when you know what the standard is, what par is, what the score is that you operate to your own greatest effectiveness in all your relations.

3. To use the ability of each employee as fully as possible by work assignments in line with individual interests, aptitude, and experience, and by recognition of constructive ideas and suggestions.

This is the old round peg in a square hole. Business

institutions now recognize that some people are good in one job and not in another and that accident isn't going to control whether a person is a failure or a success. We have at last learned enough to want to find out the greatest capabilities of the individual so that he can be helped, encouraged, put in the right place, and developed to his greatest capacity.

The greatest achievement any of us can have is the discovery and use of unexpected capabilities from among our people, even if it means that we will lose them as they go on in other fields or into a superior position.

We need all the enlightenment of an enlightened age in this field of determining the elements of each job, and the jobs of supervision come first in our attention. Some months ago I arranged for the appointment of a committee to state the responsibilities and authorities that are common to all supervision. Every single one of us has at some time been up against the stark madness of being held responsible without having the authority. We have to know where we stand, and mature people are glad to know. It gives them freedom and flexibility and greater opportunity.

4. To encourage individual growth and development for both improvement of present performance and promotion.

In this whole area of discovery of what your authority and responsibility are and what can be done to help you in the performance of these jobs, the end motive is to make of each supervisor a happier, better human being and citizen and a more productive, more successful, and better-compensated supervisor. That's the end that we're trying to seek, and to fulfill those objectives we must, as I have said, use all the tools we can get.

One of the most amazing experiences I have had is finding a man who is willing but uninformed about his job. I once had a foreman who was excellent on figures but he just could not move further in the job. I got concerned about it, and took the time to learn that he was fearful of failure because he had never had a certain amount of formal education. We arranged for him to go to night school and earn a degree, and then he went right up. It's that sort of thing which we want to find out and do.

5. To maintain fair pay by considering job requirements, prevailing salaries for similar work in other organizations, and job performance.

Now, while I sincerely believe that no man or woman works for money alone, I'm not guilty of any self-delusion. The paycheck is a very vital and important part of our lives. It's our livelihood, it's what pays the bills, it's what feeds us and clothes us and provides shelter, takes care of our families, and we mean to have our pay standards and scales fair. This does not mean that we have any money to throw away. But we're going to be fair and we're going to do everything in our power to be as sure as human beings can be of that fairness.

Within the past few months, our Salary Committee has presented recommendations for improving our job evaluation system. As nearly as I can find out, the system is out of date, complicated, and characterized more by exceptions than by observances. We're going to create a simpler, better-organized, fairer system of classification.

Here again it will not limit you in your own recognition of merit of your people. It will do just the opposite. It will provide a greater range for you to recognize merit.

6. To maintain a benefit program that provides each employee with the opportunity to protect himself against the major economic uncertainties of life.

This, of course, is a field of primary obligation, certainly for a life insurance company. We can't be going out across the land selling group benefits and do an inadequate job for our own people, and we are not going to. I was delighted at the fine results brought about through the improvement in group life benefits, and I'm confident that we soon will be able to announce substantial improvements in our pension system. Then we will want to turn to our other welfare benefits for review and improvement.

7. To maintain working conditions conducive to health, comfort, and efficiency.

That is a large order, but it's something we don't have to talk very much about. Everybody who has been in the navy knows what a happy ship is and who is responsible for it. Everybody knows what a happy home is and who is responsible for it. Everybody who has been in the army knows what a happy company street is and who is responsible for it. This business of accepting that responsibility is a matter of individual conscience and it's a very real and difficult obligation.

May I just make one further observation on this. The first few hours of an employee's relationship with us are very, very precious. There, the greatest opportunity possible exists to open the human relations we talked about on a sound, good, cordial basis. Not a sentimental basis, but one of human understanding.

8. To give clear information to each employee about job duties, job performance, and, to the greatest extent practicable, the policies and activities which affect him.

This is the principle that deals with the basic problem of communication. You can't begin to have satisfactory relations with your fellow human beings with whom you're spending most of your life if you don't have reasonably good communications—and that's a two-way street.

There is a story which illustrates what I mean. The foreman said, "Dig a hole here." The man dug it, the foreman looked at it, and said, "Fill it up and dig it here." The man dug it, the foreman looked in it, and said, "Fill it up and dig it here." The man held up his hands and said, "I quit!" You see, the foreman had forgotten to tell him he was looking for a pipe. That's important. If you're going to have a man out digging holes, you ought to tell him what he's looking for and why it's important to find it. There isn't a job in this company that isn't important, and the man who holds it will appreciate that the more he knows about his job.

9. To emphasize continuously the interdependence of individual employees, units, and departments of the company.

No man is an island. He is part of the mainland. None of us could achieve anything alone. Every single person in this room is dependent on every other person for his success, his well-being, his happiness, and his advancement. Only by cooperation can we make this great organization greater. And cooperation is not a thing you do because somebody tells you to do it. It's something that you do because you want to do it. I'd like to feel that as we leave this meeting we're moving into a new climate where we want to do it, where we want to take advantage of the skills of our staff, where we want the line to accept full human responsibilities, where we glory in the opportunity to improve and develop and lead people to better positions, to a greater state of happiness and well-being.

Last February, when the agency managers met, one of them in a speech referred with pride and satisfaction to the fact that Henry Baldwin Hyde, founder of this company, was a life insurance agent. When it came my turn to speak, I could not pass up the opportunity of reminding the people who were there that while Mr. Hyde was a life insurance agent and a very good one, he was also the actuary, he wrote the policies, he invested the proceeds, he fixed the rates, he paid the claims, he hired the help, he kept the books, he sold the stock, he figured and computed and paid the dividends, and he cooperated with himself real good!

Now, our concern in this vast institution must be to capture that spirit of cooperation which is so easy for a single individual but so difficult for groups of individualists. Let's agree that, subject to all of the mortal human problems that beset us all each day, we will make of ourselves, for our own people, examples of good will, understanding, and cooperation.

Private Management—
A Public Trust

I should like to make two points about our business system. First, a business must succeed economically. A bankrupt business helps no one. A moment's reflection brings the realization that business success results in reduced prices, increased standards of living, and more and more leisure time for creative, educational, and cultural activities. Successful business enterprises preserve the economy, keep trade moving and employment high.

Thus, profit is a good word. The optimum contribution which business can make to society—indeed, one of the highest obligations of business to society—is the creation of surplus capital which follows profitable operations.

It is this surplus which provides a major part of the

Combined from speeches before the American Gas Association in 1957 and Equitable sales managers in 1961.

funds for research, which makes possible the expansion of existing businesses and the creation of new business. This surplus supports education and nourishes our manifold cultural, spiritual, and philanthropical institutions.

My second point is that business must serve the public welfare. Indeed, it is only through public service that profit is derived. No business can long endure if the public loses confidence in the reliability of the representations or products of that business. The larger the responsibility and the greater the field of service obligation, the clearer it is to the thoughtful manager that the public interest must come first. As a man's responsibilities increase he learns inevitably that he must act with an increased sense of responsibility.

It follows that the bigger a business is, the greater is the necessity for earning and deserving public confidence and esteem through serving the best interests of the public. Big business is under suspicion and attack, not because men in big companies are bad and men in small companies good, but because there is widespread fear that bigness, which has power, will abuse its power.

These fears, I think, would be considerably mitigated if it were also generally recognized that the source of authority, particularly in big concerns, comes from below. In our nation the people are sovereign. Every business enterprise exists only because it was permitted to be created under laws enacted by the state or nation through the legislative process created by the people.

Every business manager also knows that, while appointment of official position comes from a superior or a board of directors, that appointment must be continually confirmed and reconfirmed by the official's subordinates for the authority to be exercised effectively. A business manager's authority actually comes from his subordinates and he exercises that authority as a result, in truth and in fact, of the consent of those subordinates. An appreciation of these circumstances brings, it seems to me, a healthy sense of humility.

As the age of American abundance continues, as our business life and methods become more and more complex and vast in scope and responsibility, the bigger will some of our business units grow. This is so because experience shows, and will continue to show, that there are great economic advantages to bigness. It is only the large concerns that can do certain of the big jobs in the hour of national need. It is the large companies that provide the vast sums needed for successful research on the frontiers of advancing knowledge. We who have responsibilities in large enterprises must resolve to accept a sense of stewardship and to avoid the abuse of our power and thereby keep for America the manifest economic advantages of bigness.

Now, let us ask: Does the life insurance industry serve the public interest? With more than 130 million Americans holding life insurance policies representing over a trillion dollars of insurance in force, all I can say is that we had better serve the public interest. Of course we do! The life insurance industry has for generations been regarded as a business affected with a public interest, and it has consequently been regulated by public authority. The life insurance industry is the greatest public service instrument in our national life.

I submit that our industry provides the best-known vehicle by which a man can protect and secure the human beings most precious to him against the financial hazards of life and death. Our industry stands for the most scrupulous preservation of the savings of policy owners through the prudent investment of those savings. By such investment we soundly nourish the economy of our nation. Indeed, our industry serves the fundamental human needs of millions of people—who are the public.

It is thoughts such as these which led me to state in writing the fundamental purpose, the business objectives and the goals of The Equitable. The statement constitutes a basic creed—a creed that is always subject to change and improvement. I should like to summarize the basic substance of this statement and thus share our management creed with you.

We start with the technical purpose: to provide on a scientifically sound, demonstrably fair, and economically attractive basis mutual insurance protection against financial hazards which people encounter because of disability and uncertainty as to length of life.

There are also inherent deeper and less tangible purposes. The Equitable is fundamentally a great public service institution. It is engaged in one of the most important of human activities. Its mission is to maintain and protect the security of American citizens and the American home.

But The Equitable is a business—its medium is money. While it fills great human roles, it does so by material means. Basic measurements of business success must be made in material terms. Businesses are significantly more effective if they are growing, virile, and successful.

However, we have the duty to make sure that our growth financially is always consistent with the maintenance and enhancement of our services to our policyholders. Therefore we must hold before us the dual objective of material growth and high quality of service.

The business objectives are three. First, to sell to all Americans sound life and health insurance and annuity contracts, of kinds and in amounts appropriate for their needs and means. Second, to conserve Equitable insurance in force and to administer all policies and contracts efficiently, equitably, and economically. And third, to invest reserve funds arising from insurance and annuity contracts securely, productively, and for the benefit of the American economy.

To fulfill these business objectives we must first provide a business organization which means management and manpower at all levels and a sound workable organization structure. The manpower must be carefully recruited, adequately trained, fairly compensated, ably directed, and effectively motivated. Conscious efforts must continuously be made to train and develop successors for all supervisory personnel having managerial responsibilities. We must, of course, provide comfortable and efficient facilities and working quarters to the end that our service may be economical and efficient and to the further end that our employees and agents may have high pride in the physical representation of the institution with which they have thrown their lot.

An effective organization structure must operate pursuant to acceptable and enlightened management ideals, procedures, and principles. The institution must have a management philosophy conducive to sound growth and continuing betterment which is recognized and respected by all of its members. There must be, in short, a management philosophy which includes a personnel policy based upon the reward of competence and upon respect for the sanctity and dignity of the individual human being. Authority and responsibility must be extensively delegated with minimum restrictions. Freedom to experiment within reason is requisite to individual advancement and business recovery.

The management of a large mutual life insurance company is not that of a proprietor. Our motive is not profit in the general commercial or industrial sense, but rather a sound and efficient operation achieving the greatest good for society.

The professional manager of a large privately operated, although government-regulated, public service corporation finds his important opportunity for satisfaction (1) in furnishing high-quality insurance protection at low net costs, (2) in conserving all Equitable insurance and annuity contracts, (3) in succeeding competitively, and (4) in participating in the relative growth of the enterprise.

Our growth must look well and be superior when compared to that of the industry as a whole and our natural competitors and not only when compared to that in our own past history.

An overall purpose, a business objective, an organization structure, and a philosophy of management simply set the stage. We now have work to do!

We must design, price, and administer policies. Our net cost must be equitably determined and competitive, and must soundly recognize the relative requirements of initial premium, dividend, and net cost.

We must strive to develop the ability to forecast the economic and social environments of the future and recognize future trends in their formative stage, to the end that we can act to meet or condition the future and not simply wait to react to it after the event.

Recognizing that life insurance must be sold, we need a strong and reliable marketing organization. Steps must be taken to do everything we jointly can to build an established sales organization which is superior—superior in education and experience, superior in dedication, superior in training, and composed of full-time, life-time agents.

The life insurance policies issued by the Equitable must be sold, distributed, and serviced so as to assure maximum protection for the public at minimum cost. Our operations must be economical if we are to attain our competitive goals. This commanding injunction must transcend words. We must act.

These plans and goals are not arbitrary or capricious. They are based on careful decisions—not only as to ultimate goals but as to subordinate supporting programs. It's through the determination of these subordinate policies that we convert a general goal into a concrete dollar objective. And there has been no more thrilling experience to me as a businessman than to see these abstract goals turned into reality as we implement our specific programs.

Thoughtful men are daily confronted with a gnawing

concern as to their individual contributions to the furtherance of the American ideal. Doubts creep in and question whether America has a purpose. We are blessed since we can believe in the high human and economic importance of a mutual life insurance company.

No one of us in all probability can make a greater contribution to the fulfillment of the American ideal and to the demonstration that America has a noble purpose than by the daily performance of our jobs, by together resolving individually to fulfill the best that is in each of us and to see that our performance meets the highest of standards.

Business and
the Liberal Mind

Today, in this world of multiple choice, there is considerable evidence that substantial numbers of students have a relatively poor opinion of business, particularly big business. Now, there are many students who do not have that opinion. But this morning I want to talk with those who do, and about the implications of that point of view for education and for business itself. I want to talk about those who find no challenge in business—no fulfillment of instinctive ideals; who are convinced that businessmen are preoccupied with materialistic considerations—that businessmen are sadly wanting in basic values, absorb the dollar profits, and have no concern for social values.

I think there are several basic reasons why these opin-

First delivered at Commencement of Hampden-Sydney College in 1962; later adapted and expanded for numerous college audiences.

ions are held. In the first place, the times in which we live certainly carry seeds of doubt, cynicism, possibly despair, and certainly confusion. I don't wonder that students are confused. I know I am—bitter poverty rubbing elbows with affluence; the ghastly, persistent, pervading fear of nuclear war; the religious ethic in conflict with the marketplace; the concern that the increase in knowledge on all fronts is directed not to the public good, but to its exploitation.

The second reason is that many people do not really understand the current philosophy of business—what it is that large and growing numbers of enlightened businesses seek, and why. There are many at fault in this lack of understanding, particularly business itself.

The third reason, I suggest, is that the students of America today are educated to have doubts and to express them; and this, I submit, is a very valuable quality.

Business is concerned with dollar profits, necessarily so; but it is long-term dollar profits that business is concerned with and not the quick buck—not the enrichment of the fly-by-night operator. Profits are a measure of the public's judgment of an enterprise, much as the vote is a measure of confidence in our government. A nonprofit business has more difficulty measuring its performance than a profit-making one. As the head of a mutual life insurance company, I know what I am talking about. We struggle hard to find the standard that will tell us whether we are doing all that our policyholders have a right to expect. I confirm, too, that organization, specifically "business structure," is here to stay. There simply isn't any other way to run things in a world where the population now exceeds 3½ billion people who have requirements for food, housing, transportation, education—to say nothing of intellectual and spiritual needs which defy estimate.

Harvey Cox, in his challenging book, *The Secular City*, calls our age "the age of organization" and says that ". . . our freedom in the age of organization is a question of the responsible control and exercise of power . . . for the common welfare." It would be naïve to think that government and the academic world operate today without the apparatus or organization or the threat of misuse of power which some see operating only in the world of business.

It's widely repeated that business holds no challenge for the imaginative, idealistic young man who feels the call, the urge, to serve his fellow man. But I ask you to believe me that there is plenty of challenge in business today and in a variety of types.

Consider for just a moment the implications of the simultaneous tasks faced by business management: to serve the best interests of employees, owners, and the public, including customers, to their satisfaction. An illustration: We have—as is true, I suppose, in all large business organizations—the anxious, nagging problem of the marginal employee—the man or woman who has worked year after year and still is five or ten years from retirement but is comparatively nonproductive. It is unfair to continue with that person in terms of the rights of other employees, in terms of the funds for which you are responsible, and in terms of efficiency. It is heart-warming to consider the thought and effort and care which go into identifying these people and finding a place for them where they can be happy and productive either in or outside of the company. And it touches your heart to have this responsibility in your hands.

Or consider, for example, the frequently discussed matter of the introduction of automation. All of you have heard and read of the dire predictions of widespread unemployment as the result of automation. We have revolutionized our work processes by the application of electronic data processing machines and we have eliminated literally hundreds of low-level repetitive jobs. How does one reconcile with the human values the hard-headed competitive pressures that force this technological change, specifically where it concerns the individuals whose jobs disappear? I doubt if any insurance company has proceeded further with electronic data processing than we have—yet we have guaranteed continued employment for all our people affected, and we have made good on that pledge.

One final example. What has business done to solve the most difficult and most explosive problem our country faces—the problem of a fair deal for minority groups? For a considerable time it must be admitted that business, like the rest of the community, closed its eyes and dragged its feet. But business is awake now. Big business after big business, and Equitable, thank heavens among the first, has joined the effort. We pledged ourselves that employment, and in fact all decisions that affect a person's job, will be based on job skill, experience, performance, education, and training. No quotas will be set in selecting members of a particular racial or religious group.

There is, I submit, no field of activity where human

rights and values are better recognized and more sincerely served than in business management. There is one principle of employer-employee relations that transcends every individual human right of every individual employee. The individual employee is the indispensable unit of business. Accomplishments are made by people, not by things. The enlightened businessman knows that where a genuine respect for each individual can capture an organization, the effect is far-flung and the strength of the business greatly enhanced. More than that, he knows that such respect is in fact a moral imperative.

It has been suggested from time to time that business is not really interested in liberal arts graduates whose education has not been highly specialized—that it wants only technicians and scientists. That would be like saying that Equitable wants only actuaries. We need far more than actuaries to run an insurance business. We need people to sell insurance, provide service, pay claims, invest funds, and so forth.

It is important both for us and for you to understand why business must have a steady flow of liberal arts school graduates. A few characteristics of the liberally educated graduate reveal how important they are to business for practical business reasons. Indeed, these characteristics could perhaps be described as subtle qualifications for business success.

First, there is the ability to pick assistants to whom you can confidently delegate vital responsibility. The heart of effective delegation lies in understanding how others think. The power to think and to understand the thinking of others, developed by a study of the liberal disciplines under trained scholars, is at the very heart of liberal education and it is likewise the fundamental of business success.

A second characteristic of high-quality business leadership is the capacity to distinguish between the important and the unimportant every hour, every day, every week, every year. And that's an exacting task. It takes a lot of capacity. Many mistakes have to be made before that capacity is developed.

Every business consists of an endless series of questions to be answered and problems to be solved. There are two steps to the answer to every question. The historical step is first. What are the facts? Not the facts as you think they are or wish they were, hope they are, or even as perhaps they ought to be—no. What are the facts? And secondly there is the philosophical step. What are the values that you are going to use in exercising and making a judgment upon those facts? What are your standards of values? Who is your god?

Now, you can't take a book off the shelf and find satisfactory standards or continuing criteria of values. There is no magic formula. It isn't written in any book. And there are no standards of what is always true, right, just, and beautiful. Every man and woman must develop his and her own measurement tool and criteria of values on the basis of education, environment, spiritual convictions, and daily experience. You fix your own standards of value by finding them and using them.

It is well recognized that liberal education leads the student inexorably to a study and understanding of those high principles and accepted standards which have guided men throughout the ages.

The third and last subtle qualification for success in business is the development of a capacity to differentiate between principle and expedience. This makes use of the scale of values to which I have just referred. This is the ability to apply values through action. One cannot and must never compromise with principle. But in business the point is to make principle useful, to make it work. Business must produce products and services, not reports. It must choose between alternatives, not merely describe them. Business must use principle as a sanction for action and not as an excuse for avoiding action. In this sense, business does make principle expedient.

Let me illustrate from my own business experience as a utility executive. There came a day in a large northern city when it was realized that the people could not have their homes economically heated with gas unless in some way we were able to bring vast stores of gas to the market during the warmer months and store it near the market for use during the winter months of higher demand. The engineers and geologists assured us that in a nearby geological structure, a dome, we could store millions and millions of cubic feet of gas by pumping the gas down against the salt-water sands and pushing back the water, thereby holding the gas in the dome.

Thus the application of engineering principles to our problem gave us a green light, but there was no way we could know whether that structure would really hold gas until we actually tried it. The difficulty was that there was no way to try it just a little. We had to spend millions of dollars drilling wells and installing plant and introducing billions of cubic feet of gas into the dome. We were given faith and courage to do so by wise and mature men who trusted principle and asserted emphatically that the need of the public was so great that we dared not refuse to take the risk, even at the risk of our own jobs and futures.

Now what does all this prove? I submit that it shows that the successful practice of business means fundamentally the selection, the development, the inspiration, and the advancement of men and women of high principle and a thirst for action. Men with a broad enough view to make a success of the enterprise and of themselves, and also to successfully provide service acceptable to the public in matters entrusted to their care.

In other words, any apprehension on the part of the liberal arts graduate that as a businessman he would have no opportunities to grapple with and contribute to the solution of socially significant problems is based on a false and limited view of business. Within twenty-five to fifty years society is going to bear little resemblance to the society you people have grown up in, let alone to the one people my age have known. The need for brilliant people, and especially for moral people, in business is already great and this need is increasing at a pace that makes denying business its share of liberal arts students a very serious matter indeed.

The Dignity of Selling

It has often been said that "the success of salesmen will determine largely the prosperity, happiness, and the peace of the whole world." Although this observation may be more optimistic than it is precise, I join in the belief that without effective salesmanship a free industrial society cannot long exist and prosper.

The fundamental task of the salesman is to make his prospect change. He introduces new ideas and asks his prospective client to reconsider the *status quo*. He uncovers new needs and brings old ones into focus. He points out new uses for old products and shows how new products will meet old needs. Selling thus provides the stimulus to change. But people typically do not want to be disturbed. They tend to resist change. Therefore,

Excerpted from an address before the Sales Executives Club, New York City, in April, 1968.

it is not surprising that the salesman, who is called upon to disturb, suffers, in substantial measure, rejection as well as acceptance.

In a society which is much concerned with the material here and now, the life insurance salesman presents a product (a policy or annuity contract) which is both intangible and future-oriented—a product which has no patents, no franchises, nor any special characteristics that cannot be duplicated by all competitors. Such conditions make for open competition. As a result, the life insurance salesman must truly excel in the art of salesmanship.

The life insurance agent also faces the intriguing challenge of causing people to think about and deal with highly personal, even sensitive areas of their lives. A good life insurance agent must boldly intrude upon such private areas in order to do a full and satisfactory job of insurance programming. Thus, the agent asks his prospect to reassess his own financial situation, to consider his responsibilities and relations to his loved ones, to face up to the fact that the time of his death is an uncertain and unpredictable matter, and to take stock of his own place in his environment. All of us regard such matters as intimate, highly personal, and often distressing. Quite naturally, we tend to sweep them under our emotional rugs. As a consequence, the problem confronting the life insurance salesman is somehow to make his prospect consider with care each one of these intimate and often threatening subjects.

Perhaps some of these highly intimate considerations may over time become easier for an individual to explore on his own; but the probabilities are great that life insurance contracts, and all security programs, will have to be sold by agents who have encouraged their clients to think realistically about topics which will continue to be both seriously threatening and extremely personal. It is a rare man who, on his own, is able to initiate such considerations and reach appropriate resolutions.

Today the sales forces of the life companies are being carefully and thoroughly renovated. Most companies now insist upon well-educated, fully committed and dedicated men and women who can deal with such matters efficiently and with great dignity. The future of the life insurance industry is clear in this one regard; we shall continue to face a constant demand for good life insurance agents to take our products to the public.

From where I sit, the relationship between a salesman and his prospect is essentially an exercise in human communication. A good salesman simply must be a good communicator. Correspondingly, it seems to me that failure in selling often is no more than a failure to communicate.

The word communication comes from the Latin word *communis* which means "commonness." When we communicate, we are attempting to establish some degree of "commonness" with another person or with our prospect.

In the case of selling life insurance, the communication between an agent and his prospect is fraught, as has been suggested, with special difficulties. Consequently it is especially important that we take advantage of the knowledge about communication already available to us. For example, it has been determined scientifically that:

—the more trusted the source of a message, the more readily the message will be accepted;

—the more balanced the message, the more likely it is to be effective;

—the higher the educational level of the audience, the more important it is for the communicator to be completely fair and to give all sides of the argument;

—the more threatening the message, the less likely it is to be believed;

—the greater the involvement of the audience in the topic of the communication, the more receptive the audience is likely to be;

—the greater the acceptance of a message, the stronger the tendency is to receive additional messages which support the new position;

—the lower the self-esteem of the audience, the more resistant it tends to be.

We take such research clues seriously for, if nothing else, they show that the fast-talking, shallow-thinking, quick-buck artist is no longer an accurate prototype of the successful American salesman.

Since the life insurance agent is called upon to bring repressed topics to the surface, it is easy to understand why he seems to be chronically susceptible to the development of a negative self-image. In our business, the remedy for this problem is peculiarly a managerial function—for the sales manager to be just as sensitive to the needs of his salesman as the salesman is to the needs of his clients.

Let me elaborate, very briefly, simply by reminding you of the essential loneliness of man. How easy it is for us to forget this painful characteristic which *all human beings* share, at some time and to some degree. And yet how easy it is, if it has once become part of our daily way of life, to give encouragement and support to others suffering under a like burden. A few minutes spared at the right time and in the right place for real communication between the manager and his salesman pays, as you well know, handsome dividends.

This is not just homespun philosophy—rather, this powerful force of expressed loyal support and strong backing has been identified and incorporated into highly respected theories of behavioral science. The support which one person can give to another has, in fact, been recognized as a keystone in understanding human behavior in a wide range of terrifying situations. It has been effectively utilized to understand why soldiers go into battle despite the strangling taste of fear in their mouths and the most devastating of visceral sensations; how alcoholics come to regain their self-esteem after months and even years of darkness and pain; how varsity teams have been brought to unprecedented performances with no standouts or individual stars; how young hoodlums—with no perceptible commitments to either family or society—have been transformed into self-respecting and productive citizens.

This is a principle of considerable power and one of great relevance to the business of selling. Somehow we must learn how to tap this source of support, to make it part of our managerial philosophy, and to build it permanently into our sales organizations. To be sure, the principle is implicit in the teamwork aspect of the traditional sales campaign. It is implicit in the practice of joint selling, when this is undertaken—in part, at least— to give a man a boost. And it is implicit in all kinds of organizational activities which encourage a sense of belonging and personal worth—formal recognition, conferences, informal parties, celebrations, seminars, and the small gesture or brief word of encouragement.

My own company, I believe, appreciates the importance and power of a good salesman. We rely exclusively upon the individual life insurance agent to take our products to the public. Therefore, we are vitally concerned with the success of the individual agent.

I submit that no activity is more essential to the success of a company, an industry—indeed, a national economy—than selling. In my view, selling is the basic link between production and consumption: Production gives form to the product or service; consumption, on the other hand, is the utilization of the product or service to satisfy a human need or desire. A producer is linked to the consumer by the salesman. Selling provides the utility of time, place, and possession to the product or service, just as production provides the utility of form and substance. The end result of planning, financing, and producing is a sale. Nothing happens until a sale is made.

We are constantly being made aware of new and exciting products; products capable of satisfying the ever-greater needs, desires, and appetites of the American people. But all these new and exciting products are of little use if they remain in the warehouse of the manu-facturer or on the shelves of the retail store. Salesmen and salesmanship are needed to put these products into use, to educate the public as to their merits and availability— to stimulate consumers to buy.

Salesmanship has frequently been called an art. It is considered an art rather than a science because it is a human skill that depends on special individual practice to a much greater extent than on general and uniform principles or procedures. In my own attempts to analyze the art of salesmanship, three elements seem to com-mand attention.

The first basic element is knowledge. The salesman must know everything about the product or service he is to sell; what it is, how it is made, how to use it, and how it measures up to the products or services of competitors. Such knowledge, of course, he learns through training, more from self-study, but perhaps, most important, from intelligent observation of what is going on around him.

The salesman must also know himself—what a chal-lenge that is! Through self-analysis he must learn his strong and his weak points. He must then strive to de-velop within himself those characteristics essential to inspire confidence and to build an effective sales per-sonality.

Further, the salesman must know his prospective buy-ers. He must analyze their needs, their concerns, and their abilities to buy. The salesman should be able to de-termine the potentials of each of his prospects even better than the prospect can himself. Finally, the salesman must know and apply the basic techniques and procedures of his own vocation. This requirement of knowledge means that perhaps more than in any other field a salesman spends his life learning and relearning his job.

The second element is creativity. Knowledge alone is not sufficient to make a person a good salesman. The good salesman works to apply knowledge to his task, and always with imagination. As a specialist in communication, the salesman must constantly fashion and redesign his presentation to suit the individual prospect and to assure maximum appeal to the buying motives of that prospect. Ingenuity is, of course, the essential ingredient.

It has been said that perhaps one man in twenty has the capability to launch out into business for himself. Many have or can acquire most of the requisite ingredients, including financial backing, but most men never take the leap because they lack a certain combination of the qualities required for success. To be successful, the independent worker must be creative, tireless, and confident. His success depends upon his ability to create opportunities for himself day after day.

In my judgment, the commission salesman is the outstanding illustration of individuality and self-sufficient independence. He is his own boss. He is rewarded with returns commensurate with his performance—no more, no less.

The third major element of salesmanship is service. This is the most important ingredient, for in the last analysis the successful salesman over the long term must primarily serve the interests of others; to be achieved over the long term his own ends must be subordinated. It is essential that the relationship between salesman and client be one of mutual trust and confidence. Persistent and dedicated service provides the only reliable assurance of the continuance of such confidence. Thorough and complete service brings, to salesman and client alike, comfort and peace of mind, together with a sense of security and economic well-being. Thus, and only thus, does the salesman work at the very center of a business enterprise.

Man, Organization,
and the Computer

I am here to express—and to try to support—a conviction that electronic data processing has taken its place as one of the everyday, standard tools of life insurance work. *Some* of us must be concerned with its technical implications, but all of us must understand its impact on our organizations—an impact that touches all of the traditional fields of management interest.

We need not be mathematicians, electronics experts, engineers, or specialists of any other kind to understand what electronic data processing means in the context of general management practice. After all, we use automobiles—and understand both what they will do *for* us and what, if we are not careful, they may do *to* us— without concerning ourselves with how the engine runs or how it is tuned up or why it is designed in a particular

Drawn principally from an address at the Life Office Management Association's automation forum in Chicago in March, 1962.

way. Business managers are fully justified in feeling the same way about the new tools of office production. There has been enough experience, in my judgment, to dispel the mysticism and establish a sound basis for confidence. A lot has been done in a few years.

It is a tribute to the imagination and vigor of the life insurance business that we were among the very first to see the possibilities, and have consistently been leaders, in applying the new technology to office operations. This is, however, no more than should be expected of us. In many enterprises, office work supports the production line, and automation of this office work is, in a sense, secondary to automation of the factory or the plant. For us, automation of our office work *is* automation of the production line.

There are, however, broad problems of policy that face the management of a life insurance company which go beyond the areas of technical specialization in their general impact: problems, for example, of personnel, organization, environmental change, and so on.

The impact of EDP on individual employees must continue to have our attention. The genesis of the problem is obvious: When manual operations are replaced by machine procedures, the result is to reduce clerical jobs below the number that would otherwise be required. With cost reduction as a major goal, there has to be constant emphasis on achieving the planned reduction in job positions. Under these circumstances, it is only natural that the first concern of individual employees is with their own futures. We must be sure that this concern is recognized and allayed. To do otherwise would depart from our industry's tradition of bringing about progress in office practices without harm to our employees' interests; it would also result in our lacking the cooperation of the very men and women whose help is essential in making the change.

As I believe has been quite generally the case, we have assured all employees many times that no one will lose his or her job as the result of the electronics program. Normal turnover, particularly at the levels where EDP is likely to cut in the most, actually accounts for many more resignations in a year than we can possibly match in specific jobs eliminated by automation. The growth of our business, both in volume and in scope, is continually opening up new jobs. The electronics activity itself accounts for new opportunities in the fields of systems design, programming, and machine operations. For all of these reasons, the problem of displacement, measured in terms of aggregates, is not a difficult one.

Such a conclusion is not enough by itself. We must look beyond the aggregates at each individual employee, and find a specific new place for each man or woman in an area undergoing change. This can be difficult, and it often is. Employees whose jobs in one part of the company are affected by EDP are not always the most suitable or best qualified for openings created by expansion in another part. Normal turnover rarely matches exactly the timing and extent of job reduction stemming from a particular stage in the transition to EDP. We have found no general solution to the problem; we have simply made sure that a responsible senior person takes account of each case and keeps at it until the right answer is found.

Beyond the question of direct job security, there are more subtle questions of management concern arising from the fact that almost everyone in an area affected by EDP finds his or her pattern of work changed in some way. The change may be minor—getting used to a new arrangement of information on a previously familiar report, for example—or it may be so large that the individual concerned finds that he really has a new job. In the latter case, the situation is usually foreseen and will be planned for in advance. But one of the major causes of tension comes from the large number of cases of the first kind which all too easily get overlooked and which, until they are assimilated, cause rough going.

No matter how carefully planned, a major change requires a period of adjustment. In this, the atmosphere of overall confidence is particularly important. Often, the ultimate success of a new way of doing things depends on people of long experience whose confidence in their mastery of the work at hand may temporarily be weakened. We must reassure them that their knowledge of our business, our traditions, and our practices is just as valuable as ever, even though our method of getting the work done is changed. There are psychological needs that are every bit as important as the technological needs accompanying major change.

We have had to recognize, too, that the introduction of EDP may have profound effects on organization structure. Since the days when the whole job of running the company grew to be too much for one man, we have divided our work into segments and created separate organizational units to correspond to these segments. It has been the right course, in the past, to departmentalize function by function. Now we are faced with a reversal: Electronic data processing equipment gives the best overall results when related functions are integrated to the greatest possible degree. The effect is to create new conditions within which those who are responsible for organization structure must make their plans.

To illustrate one approach to these new conditions, let me summarize what The Equitable has done. Our first electronics work was concentrated in the area of individual insurance administration, and some years ago we changed our departmental organization to fit in better with the new systems that were being developed. In our structure, a department is the major operating organizational element. We formed a new department, combining elements from several existing departments, in order to place under one head the various functions that would be closely related in the EDP procedures developed for the administrative work. This pattern has been followed by other changes in operating alignments as our program has developed.

These steps have been taken at the start of each major phase of development, sometimes months or even years before the expected date of implementation. It has seemed to us to be most important that those who are eventually to have the operating responsibility for the success of the new methods should, from the beginning, have full authority in the making and carrying out of the transition plans and the personnel arrangements.

On the other hand, in organizations as complex as ours there is no such thing as isolation among departments. No matter what the alignment of functions, the department with the main operating responsibility will still be dependent in one way or another on almost all, if not all, of the company's other departments—and vice versa. We have found that one of the major effects of electronic data processing is a continual deepening of this dependence of each department's work upon the others'.

Work procedures that cross departmental lines should, under any conditions, be built upon mutual understanding and confidence; under the conditions we now face, they must be! It simply isn't possible to operate an EDP system without very close cooperation among those responsible for handling the original information and those who use the end results. It remains one of the drawbacks of even the most advanced machine that it cannot—as humans can—adjust itself to unexpected variations in the way data are handled or instructions interpreted.

Because our machines cannot adapt themselves automatically to even the smallest change from what they have been programmed to expect and deal with, we must—whenever we want to use them—learn to say precisely what we want. This is not characteristic behavior for most of us; we are more accustomed to saying approximately what we want, leaving it to those who are to carry out the work to fill in the gaps with normal imagination or, if they have to, come back and ask questions when something unexpected develops. The requirement that we know exactly what we want in advance is, of course, what underlies the point I made a moment ago in speaking of the need for a greater degree of mutual understanding among those who share responsibility for a given area of work being done by a machine.

It also means that when we want to make a change in our practices, we cannot do so until its total effect has been analyzed—not, as has often been the case in the past, after general agreement on the principles, with the details left to be worked out as we go along.

These are some of the main problems confronting management as a result of the rapid growth of electronic data processing in our companies. They are all people-oriented rather than machine-oriented. They are problems with new faces, but not really new problems.

And if we can see the problems, we can certainly see the benefits—those already being realized and those that are still to come.

We have been able to lower operating costs in the areas where EDP is well established.

We have been able to improve accuracy and reduce our exposure to clerical error.

We have been able to reduce the proportion of emotionally and intellectually unsatisfying jobs and increase the number of satisfying, creative jobs.

We have been able to take steps aimed at better service to our policyholders and field forces, and can see ways to do more.

We have been able to give our actuaries the means of accomplishing their research and developmental work more thoroughly and rapidly.

We are developing new opportunities for research in marketing, underwriting, investment analysis, and other areas.

Ours is, indeed, an industry that can continue to lead the way in applying this marvel of man's engineering ingenuity. But how well we do this does not depend on how large, or how fast, or how versatile the machines themselves may be. It depends on how competent, how well-trained, how dedicated to the goals of our business are the men and women we assign to this work. We will fail if we see the machines as ends in themselves; we will succeed if we see them, and use them with imagination, as one of the means to a larger end.

Part 3

The Society

"Inflation and Employment: A Basic Conflict" calls attention to a national dilemma, one which has torn Mr. Oates over the years. As an insurance executive, he must urge, even demand, that the value of the dollar be protected. As a human being, however, he is appalled by the waste from unemployment, especially among the young. Can the conflict be reconciled? Mr. Oates attempts an affirmative response—by demanding that both government and business fulfill their appropriate functions. And he offers for consideration a plan to subsidize the wages of unskilled labor, a program which would require new levels of flexibility and trust between government, business, and society.

The life insurance industry is the nation's largest private source of long-term capital. Historically, in making their investment decisions the companies have been concerned essentially with two criteria: safety of principal and rate of return. Today, largely due to the influence of Mr. Oates, as discussed in "Innovative Capital: A Social Force," there is an emerging third criterion, and that is social value. His ideas in this speech sparked an industry pledge of $1 billion of venture capital for investment in the inner cities. This pledge was extended a year later to include a second billion dollars.

Somewhat later after the initial billion dollars was pledged, Mr. Oates turned his attention, in a series of speeches, to the deeper consequences of the commitment. In large measure, he asked: "What are we going to do with this money? Are we going to continue to uproot people from their neighborhoods? Are we going to continue to bring in outsiders to tell the people what they should and can have? Is the majority going to continue to discriminate against the minority?" His response, in "The Urban Condition: Guidelines for Action," was to look at the problems of the cities in human terms: to "recognize all the inhabitants of the cities to be members of the community." Having done that, the guidelines are clear: to share with all inhabitants the benefits of the total community; to construct new institutions for dealing with the problems and the opportunities; to encourage broader participation in all aspects of society. Added Mr. Oates: "I feel strongly . . . that even the picketing of schools by concerned parents, and rent strikes by aroused occupants of substandard tenements, can be healthy signs."

In 1966, Mr. Oates became one of the first businessmen to speak out on that most emotional of public questions, population control. "Business and Demography: The Population Crisis" addresses itself to the potential threat that overpopulation poses to business stability; but more intently, it speaks in terms of human needs for survival and growth. In the end, Mr. Oates returns to the fundamental reference point of his beliefs: the individual. And he suggests the development of a new freedom—"the right to be born with dignity." In the years since, that point of view has won an increasing number of advocates.—B.C.B.

Inflation and Employment:
A Basic Conflict

There are two mighty problems crying for solution in our national life. The first is the destructive evil of inflation and the necessity for its control. The second is a horrendous, bitter, and violent challenge in the consequences of poverty, discrimination, and racism. Thus, there coexist ruinous inflation and urban crisis. They are interrelated and unhappily so, since the control of inflation proceeds at the risk of increasing unemployment, which falls most heavily on the urban minorities, thus aggravating their grievances, their anxieties, and their concerns.

Unless inflation can be reduced, it will be impossible for us to fulfill many other important national objectives designed to serve the needs of the underprivileged. It is

Excerpts from a speech at the 1964 symposium sponsored by The Harvard Business Review *and reprinted in the issue of September-October, 1964; material from later speeches before business audiences is also incorporated.*

the resolve and high purpose of the national administration to conquer inflation and to do so through the application of fiscal and monetary brakes, but in a gradual manner so as to minimize the danger of precipitating a recession. We seek, by some miraculous way, to provide simultaneously business growth, full employment, and stable prices. I do hope we can succeed. History, however, does not indicate that these simultaneous objectives can be easily achieved. Somehow or other, business must take measures in collaboration with government which will have the effect of tempering the rise of unemployment as the economy cools. We must be realistic enough to recognize that fiscal and monetary restraints will not long be acceptable or tolerable if progress in the control of inflation involves the accelerated unemployment of the minority peoples, the poor and the bitter, those who are least able or willing to accept such consequences.

In dealing with this complicated problem, private industry has an essential role to play in helping to train and find useful job opportunities for the disadvantaged. Not one company, not one industry alone can make much of an impact; but if American business in its entirety can be aroused to accept the responsibility, its united efforts cannot help but make a significant contribution.

We at The Equitable have been working hard to change our internal hiring policies. As late as 1960, there were still few minority-group salaried employees at Equitable. Now, nationwide, some 13.5 per cent of such employees are representatives of minority groups. In the Home Office here in New York, the figure is about 20 per cent and this is certain to rise. Of those currently being hired in New York City, 60 per cent are Negro and Puerto Rican. Every Equitable office throughout the country is integrated, including the South.

At present more than 200 agents out of a sales force of more than 7,000 are from a minority group. There are 20 Negro district managers out of some 400. The manager of one of the Philadelphia agencies is a Negro, as are the managers of agencies in Los Angeles and Chicago.

In addition, our Home Office in New York City is now in its sixth year of training high school dropouts, largely Negroes, for jobs. The program is not a complete success, but there have been substantial accomplishments that make it well worth the effort.

In view of the very grave problem of youth unemployment, we ought to take a look at our state and national minimum wage laws and ask whether they are contributing to the high unemployment rates among youth. I am fully aware that minimum wage legislation has served to eliminate many labor abuses, and I do not in any way suggest its repeal. What I am saying is that we must reexamine these laws with particular reference to their impact on unemployed youth.

This is not a new concern of mine. When I served as a member of President Kennedy's Committee on Youth Employment, I attempted to induce recognition of the relationship between minimum wages and youth employment. For each time the minimum wage rate is raised or applied to additional job classifications, businessmen are given a financial incentive to eliminate jobs. They are stimulated to cut services or to substitute machines in order to keep their price structure competitive. Is it not inevitable that this powerful negative incentive must result in denying job opportunities to many people, particularly the unskilled, untrained young workers?

As I have indicated, I do not suggest the repeal of the minimum wage laws. What I am saying is that we should explore measures to ensure that the burden of these laws shall not fall entirely on one harassed and desperate minority—the unemployed youth. At the very least, we should go slowly in raising or expanding such legislation any further until we understand more clearly its true impact on employment.

As a first step in the process of clarifying our thinking, we should admit frankly that we cannot expect the private sector of a profit-motivated economy to pick up the tab for the subsidized employment of young and untrained labor. Exhortation by government to businessmen about their social responsibilities may produce no more than a token impact on the numbers of unemployed. A businessman's first responsibility is to the owners of his business. We cannot ask or expect him to use stockholders' assets to employ labor at rates above its true value to the enterprise. If the minimum wage laws are, in fact, an obstacle to the private employment of marginal labor, we must examine the available alternatives: either to modify the laws or to pay the subsidy necessary to cover the differential between labor's true economic value and the minimum legal rates.

The subsidy route is the direction in which much current thinking obviously is moving. Most recent proposals involve subsidies for education, subsidies for job training, and subsidies for employment on public projects. The Youth Conservation Corps proposals are a form of subsidized labor on public projects.

I take a dim view of most of the proposals for subsidized employment on public projects, because there is no future in such activities. We cannot permanently support large numbers of people entirely on the public payroll. At the end of two years in the parks or woods, the boys still would be, in large measure, ill-equipped to find jobs in our competitive society. These conservation proposals have popular public appeal because of the feeling that the boys would be doing constructive work in the woods in a healthy environment. I submit that we could buy far more parks, forests, and recreation facilities if but a small fraction of the money involved in these proposals were turned over to the forest rangers and the park superintendents to buy and improve the wilderness.

No, I fear that we cannot solve this problem by shipping the boys off to the woods.

What we need today is to find constructive employment in the private sector of our economy. We must open the doors of opportunity and accept these boys and girls as part of our labor force. They must be given the discipline of regular work habits. They must be given exposure to opportunities for advancement and encouraged to perfect their skills and talents.

I have great confidence in the ingenuity and resourcefulness of the U.S. businessman. If he is given access to a supply of labor, priced at its true economic value, he will quickly devise ways of using it effectively. He will not only use it; he will also train it with skills that will offer increasing opportunities for future advancement.

There are two principal ways that might be used to subsidize this marginal labor in private employment. One method would be to use a federal income tax incentive; the other would be a direct payroll subsidy. I rather suspect that the tax approach would be the easier to administer and perhaps would be the more acceptable politically.

We already have precedent for the tax method in the investment credit which was incorporated in the 1962 revenue bill. The purpose of this feature was to encourage capital investment in plant and equipment as a stimulant to more growth and job opportunities. I see no compelling reason why a similar tax credit could not be offered to employers who make payroll expenditures at the legal minimum rates for certain carefully defined classes of unskilled, marginal labor whose employment we seek to encourage.

An even more direct approach would be an outright cash payroll subsidy to employers who provide new jobs for these young people at the minimum rates. It would certainly be forthright and would bring out in the open the true costs of the program. The appropriation bill could readily require an annual reappraisal by Congress, at which time the classes covered and the levels of support could be altered as required.

I do not minimize the administrative difficulties which would be inherent in such a program. Whatever the difficulties, they do not appear to be insuperable; but I recognize that far more study is needed before the idea can be considered administratively feasible. Great care would need to be taken in describing types of employment eligible for the payroll subsidy to avoid having subsidized labor replace or compete with labor now being employed at the minimum wage rates. The subsidy probably should be initially limited to persons below a certain age, thus making the subsidy temporary, and to new jobs or to jobs that otherwise could not be undertaken without the subsidy.

The problem of substitution could be controlled by limiting the amount of subsidized labor that any company could employ to, say, 3 to 5 per cent by numbers of the total payroll. This percentage figure could be flexible, depending on the industry or the geographical location.

Employers located in chronically depressed areas might be permitted or encouraged to employ a much higher percentage of subsidized labor. Administrative details could also require some on-the-job training and eventual graduation into the regular, unsubsidized labor force.

A favorable feature of such a plan is that it would be relatively inexpensive. In round numbers we have about one million unemployed individuals between the ages of 14 and 19. These ages represent about 25 per cent of our total unemployed. If they were all put to work on a 40-hour work week with an average subsidy of 50 cents per hour, the total cost would amount to $1 billion annually. At 75 cents per hour the subsidy costs would still be $1.5 billion or less. These wages to newly employed teenagers would be taxable, and the government would retrieve, from the $1.5 billion expenditure, tax collections of about $200 million. In comparison, the Senate Subcommittee on Employment and Manpower has proposed an annual increase of $5 billion in the federal administrative budget to relieve unemployment. Clearly, this proposal for subsidization of wages is far less inflationary than present programs.

The total costs to our society of the payroll subsidy would be greatly reduced because the people involved would soon be contributing to the national product to the full extent of their ability, where formerly they were being supported in idleness.

Those of you who are familiar with our agricultural price support legislation will recognize that the payroll subsidy plan just outlined employs essentially the same device as the bill passed by Congress for the support of cotton prices. The cotton bill authorizes a subsidy to be paid to domestic textile mills to cover the differential between the world market price of cotton and the domestic minimum price.

But there the similarity ends. The agricultural program is an extremely wasteful one. The lion's share of the benefits go to wealthy farmers who least need public support. Poor marginal farmers get relatively little or nothing from the program. By contrast, the payroll subsidy plan would be pinpointed directly on the target.

The unknown of this labor subsidy idea is whether new and useful jobs at some price can, in fact, be found in our modern society for the unemployed, consisting, in large part, of untrained youth—including school dropouts. As I said earlier, there are some who doubt it. The existence of such doubts is not hard to understand. I believe strongly, however, that we should try to find out. If there is no place at all for the unemployed at any price, we face a truly alarming situation and the sooner we get the true facts the better. If we discover that we have a million or more permanently unemployable persons in our population, then some fresh thinking and planning will surely be required. We would certainly wish to exhaust every effort to avoid resorting to compulsory training, policed employment, or internal, massive relief.

A quick and inexpensive way of finding out would be to offer the payroll subsidy plan as a pilot project in a few typical communities of concentrated unemployment. If no jobs are offered—no subsidy. If new jobs do appear, then perhaps we will have found a hopeful and inexpensive solution to a vexing national problem.

I have deliberately sought to limit this idea to unemployed teenagers because it is considered that their problems are the most pressing. If it should prove successful in that area, it might also be considered for use as a device for easing technologically displaced adult coal miners and farmers (or others in similar positions) back into new and useful occupations.

Innovative Capital:
A Social Force

There are persuasions in life today which teach institutions of size and antiquity such as The Equitable that we've got to be prepared to embrace innovation. In the field of life insurance investments, two of these persuasions are most effective.

The first is the compelling necessity of competition. Our competitive position depends upon our net cost as much as anything else, and this is comprised basically of three items. The first is our mortality experience; this depends upon our skill as an insurance underwriter. The second is our expense of operations; this depends upon our ability as a business administrator. The third is the return on our investments, the most highly competitive element by far in the net cost picture.

Drawn from the 1967 Columbia University-McKinsey Foundation Lecture series and from numerous speeches before business audiences.

The second persuasion that leads us to accept change in the investment area is the element of social need. It is this which provides us with promising opportunities for seeking out new and imaginative ways of responding to the financial demands of our changing society. Consequently, in this discussion, the two traditional insurance investment criteria—safety and yield—will be assumed. It is the social content of our discussion that will command our primary attention.

The life companies view their investments as being in the nature of a public trust that should be scrupulously handled in the public interest. Although the rights and obligations of the parties arise from a contract and not from a trust, a social philosophy must permeate investment administration. There are, of course, times when a proposed investment may be fully eligible on grounds of safety and yield but has such dubious social values as to invite strong reservations. The case of gambling casinos is a good illustration. The life companies typically have refrained from their financing. The lines, however, are far from clear, and they are constantly changing. The distinction between a pari-mutuel racetrack, a baseball park, bingo, the legalized slot machine, and a lottery is not an obvious one.

The social, moral, and economic problems of our society are bound to become more rather than less complex. Similarly, the investment opportunities which are constantly unfolding challenge us to be responsive to the new requirements of an increasingly technological society. It is necessary to take a long, hard look to see whether our investments made today will be serving society's needs tomorrow in constructive and dynamic ways.

There is, for example, the development of the taconite mill in the production of iron. In the Mesabi Range, vast quantities of taconite and low-grade ore were being left in the ground. It was discovered, however, that it would be economically feasible to crush the taconite, extract the iron ore by a magnet, and roll it into pellets to be used in making steel. A contract with the mines was subsequently proposed to supply the taconite, and another agreement with the mills to produce the pellets for sale to the steel industry. Under this unprecedented arrangement, a group of life companies committed millions of dollars to finance the first taconite pellet plant at Silver Bay, Minnesota. Other taconite mills followed; employment and income recovered. Not only was a region saved from stagnation, but an unused resource had been put to work.

The life insurance companies also anticipated the future as reflected in the long-term debt financing of the first private atomic power plant, the facility at Rowe, Massachusetts, operated by the Yankee Atomic Electric Company.

The financing of jet planes by private airlines was another innovation in which the insurance industry played an important role. As C. R. Smith, Chairman, American Airlines, recently observed:

> Credit for the jet revolution should go to the three principal participants: the manufacturers, . . . the airlines, . . . and the financial institutions, with faith

in the enterprise and willingness to provide the long-term credits needed to finance the project.

A high percentage of the long-term loans came from the insurance companies and they should have credit for their major part in bringing about the jet revolution.

The life companies, to a degree at least, have seized opportunities to initiate and participate in investment programs that support the imaginative entrepreneur, that foster economic growth and advance the standard of living. We must serve in the future far more effectively and in a wider area as trustees of large pools of private savings to the end that they may be made boldly available for long-term investment for the capital requirements and ever-expanding needs of our entire society.

In these social respects, however, we are not without gnawing problems. I shall discuss two of these: the need for capital formation and the need for community development.

In the first place, we are desperately concerned about the nation's vital needs for future capital formation. We are today on the threshold of an enormous increase in our labor force and simultaneously the world's first trillion-dollar economy of a single nation. In 1975, our labor force will exceed 93 million persons, an increase of 15 million over the 1965 figure. The number-one challenge before us is to provide the jobs needed to employ this surging tide of manpower.

To attain this employment objective will require a huge increase in private investment, and this, in turn, is dependent upon capital formation. In one of its research studies, the National Industrial Conference Board estimates that by 1975 nonresidential fixed investment needs will require an annual expenditure of over $118 billion. This estimate indicates a need for growth in the annual rate of capital investment during the period from 1964 to 1975 that is 15 per cent higher than the expected growth during the same period in total gross national product. This means there must be jobs available, which, in turn, means we must have the economic growth that can come about only if there is adequate capital to finance the new and expanded plants and facilities so badly needed.

To form such huge quantities of capital, an important role must be accorded to the accumulation of private savings. Professor Simon Kutznets of Harvard, in his monumental study entitled *Capital in the American Economy: Its Formation and Financing,* warns:

"The demand for capital over the coming two and a half to three decades is likely to be large. . . . Under the circumstances, the supply of voluntary savings may not be adequate."

The life insurance industry, together with all other mechanisms for encouraging saving, must, it seems to me, take all possible steps to help to meet the rising need for capital funds. Consequently, we should foster close coordination and integration with federal programs and measures to the end that we are not impaired in our ability to accumulate capital. Some recent developments in Canada and Europe bear on this problem. The experience in Canada is revealing and possibly prophetic.

Following the promulgation of the recent Canadian and Quebec Government Pensions Plans, there resulted not only a negative effect on the installation of new private pension programs but, because of pension plan "cash-ins," a significantly reduced flow of funds available for investment by Canadian life insurance companies.

Our European friends are also concerned with the need to accumulate savings to promote long-term investment and economic growth. An important conference on capital markets was recently sponsored by the Atlantic Institute and the Business and Industry Advisory Council of the Organization for Economic Cooperation and Development. It was there concluded that sound economic growth requires strengthened and improved capital markets. It was further agreed that the capital markets of continental Europe must be stimulated by cooperative action among government, industry, and financial institutions, and that one of the primary policy objectives of government should be to encourage contractual savings institutions like life insurance companies and pension funds. The United States was held up as the model of a desirable capital market which accumulates savings for long-term investment from private sources and not from government as is the case in continental Europe.

Let us turn now to a second and even more pervasive problem—the need for community development. We live in a period of transition to an ever-expanding metropolitan society rather than in well-established and defined metropolitan communities. Indeed, one doesn't have to look far to find commentators who quite seriously raise the question as to whether man can develop an adequate sense of community within the impersonal, anonymous, and confusing conditions of our vast metropolitan areas. Urban sprawl, downtown blight, to say nothing of a wide range of social problems—crime, divorce, alcoholism, juvenile delinquency, drug addiction, graft, corruption—are all cited as evidences of past failures. The number and complexity of such problems will predictably increase during the next two decades. For any type of business enterprise primarily concerned with people, such as life insurance, to stand aloof from this agonizing predicament is not only unthinkable but, in fact, impossible.

To be sure, we are directly or indirectly involved in many specific programs having to do with equal employment opportunity, rehabilitation procedures, corporate citizenship, comprehensive medical care, and continuing education. But we tend, I fear, to look upon these as crash programs rather than as long-term commitments. David Rockefeller recently said of New York City, "The most important thing the big companies here can do is to stay in the city and do an efficient, profitable job." This is, of course, a basic necessity. But we should and can do more—perhaps much more.

If our social problems are great, so are our talents, our resources, and our determinations. I have no clear-cut answers or ready solutions to offer. But certainly there is much to be done both by public leaders and by private managers in enhancing still further both the quality and the level of the American standard of life. These programs must call for widening rather than limiting the areas of public and private cooperative efforts. This is especially applicable in the investment field, where private funds have served, along with tax dollars, to contribute to the development of community life. The life insurance companies have for over one hundred years attempted to serve the public interest and the needs of our society in this regard.

But, as I have suggested, the problems have become increasingly severe; and, for my part, I believe that we in the life insurance industry should engage in searching, dynamic, bold, and imaginative schemes directed toward their solution. I believe that we should espouse programs which will encourage us to invest more, to be even more experimental, to take more rather than fewer risks in the future of metropolitan America. Perhaps we need a new concept of venture capital in the social field. I do not pretend to be wise enough to know. But in the meantime, I believe that we, of the industry, can pledge our best efforts to the end that we may continue to fulfill our historic role in helping to meet the vital capital needs of the future.

The Urban Condition:
Guidelines for Action

Our future is destined to be governed to a substantial extent by our success, acting as a coalition—government, business, labor, community organizations of all kinds—in the diagnosis and cure of the sickness of our cities. This sickness is incredibly severe and pervasive. It could readily develop into a fatal blight.

As we confront this problem of great size and overwhelming complexity, it is not surprising that we are plagued by hard choices, indecisions, and doubts. This is because our approaches to the problem must also be involved and complex. Since The Equitable—along with a lengthening list of business firms—has been earnestly striving to arrive at wise decisions, I will attempt to offer a business analysis of the situation and a proposed course of action.

First delivered in Washington, D.C., in January, 1968; later adapted for business gatherings in Chicago and Pittsburgh.

In our view, the basic problem breaks down into three categories of questions: first, questions of priorities; second, questions of responsibility; and third, questions of involvement. And each of these categories, in turn, has a long list of specific and collateral issues.

Questions of priority ask *what* comes first in importance. The critical urgency of the situation and danger to society call on us to *do* something. In doing something, how should the priorities be assigned?

—What is the relative urgency of physical facilities—housing, commercial buildings, libraries—on the one hand, and on the other hand, social roles, notably jobs and educational opportunities? How much of our resources should be allocated to each?

—Another important priority issue asks whether to rebuild the blighted areas or to rehabilitate existing structures.

Secondly, the questions as to responsibility and *where* it inevitably lies raise equally perplexing issues:

—Where does public responsibility end and private enterprise begin? What are their relative roles?

—What should be the relationship between local programs (whether public *or* private) and programs to meet the larger requirements of the surrounding area or region?

Finally, the questions of involvement raise moral issues as to *who* should and must participate:

—Should the intended beneficiaries of such programs participate in their own salvation? If so, on
what basis? Is some reallocation of power and
authority to the poor a necessary condition to
resolving our urban dilemma?

—Furthermore, this question of *who* is distinctly
related to the most agonizing moral issue of our
time. Can black-white collaboration be made to
work?

It would seem to be desirable, therefore, to discuss a
sampling of issues under each of these three central questions: (1) *What* objectives come first? (2) *Where* does
the responsibility lie? (3) *Who* is to participate?

When we analyze the city from a "systems" point of
view, we discover the importance of the heart of the city.
People in the surrounding neighborhoods look to the
central city for employment, for services and shopping,
for recreation—indeed, for all the comforts and necessities of a good life. In addition to reversing commercial
and residential deterioration, revitalization of the heart
of the city is, so far as I know, the only acceptable way
of slowing down the flight to suburbia—a trend which
is creating a whole new range of national problems.

Let us consider, then, the question of priorities. In
our practical programs of urban renewal, we must think
not only of changing the physical environment; we must
not forget that it is people, after all, who make up a
city. Thus, when we lay our plans for new buildings or
new shopping centers, we must simultaneously plan for
the people who will live in those buildings or who will
shop in those centers. Research shows that the sense of

neighborhood is often so important that the best way to improve conditions may be to rehabilitate the buildings, not destroy existing structures or enforce drastic residential change upon the inhabitants. This approach enables a stable neighborhood to continue on a higher scale, but complete with its involved network of individual roles, social institutions, personal centers of influence and friendships.

Another way of supporting this point is to observe that people need a sense of identity. They need to belong. Much has been written of the difference in spirit, though not in physical surroundings, of the early Italian and Irish slums in our cities and our present ghettos. One tragic difference is that the earlier slums tended to be stable neighborhoods—places where people felt they belonged and were needed—whereas the contemporary ghetto is typically not a neighborhood but rather a collection of dilapidated buildings filled with people who have been isolated and consequently alienated. A first step toward rehabilitation, then, may very well be to restore a sense of neighborhood.

The development of physical facilities, in short, will be of little avail unless meaningful social roles are also provided, including primarily jobs. Recent experience in my own company has strongly demonstrated the importance of a job as an essential badge of membership in the larger society. Our employment of high school dropouts—largely young Negroes and Puerto Ricans—is a record of accomplishment and difficulty, joys and sorrows. On balance, however, we are more than satisfied that it is a relative success.

I commend the partnership between government and

private industry to train and to hire the unemployed. This is a measure that could go far to multiply satisfying roles and provide an enlarged sense of community. A paycheck is a passport to self-respect and self-sufficiency. I can think of nothing more rewarding for a businessman than to experience the success of a training experiment or of opening up new job opportunities. It seems to me that the field for creative thinking in this area is not only wide open but susceptible to quick results.

The question of priorities, in effect, suggests that rebuilding and rehabilitation are complementary processes, with all inhabitants of the city given the opportunity to play significant roles in the larger community.

As to *where* the responsibility lies, it is generally agreed that the nature and scope of the urban problem call for both private and public enterprise. Neither can do the job alone. And this points up the necessity of cooperative effort and open lines of communication. But a spirit of cooperation—however cordial—is obviously not enough. Not only must public and private interests share the task of rebuilding and revitalizing our cities, but equally important, there is an ever-growing need for the economic resources essential to carry out these programs. This, too, will require close coordination and integration between government and private programs, to the end that business is not impaired in its ability to accumulate adequate —indeed, vital—pools of capital.

It also seems clear that constructive urban design must be both planned and implemented within the context, not of separate cities but of vast and ever-expanding metropolitan areas. Such areas, as we all know, are made up of many disparate cities and towns. Each locality has its own government. Each strives to meet its own local interests, usually within a narrow perspective. Furthermore, local governments, quite understandably, do not wish to yield any of their prerogatives to outsiders. Yet if planning is to succeed, it requires a strong metropolitan base. This can be achieved only when local loyalties and jurisdictions give way to some higher level of authority.

The predicament of our cities is a complex of many interlocking, overlapping problems—problems of transportation, housing, education, subcultures, population change, and countless others. Each of these problems, quite understandably, has its own corps of specialists; most of us become specialists in one field or another and we tend to talk and associate only with other specialists in the same field. Yet herein lies another basic difficulty. For nothing can be more frustrating than the struggles of a group of specialists to find the solution to a general problem.

As a businessman who has seen the management team operate with some success under a variety of conditions, I believe that we must learn a great deal more about the great variety of team systems and interdisciplinary approaches to long-range urban design and community development.

One such approach to urban problems which has its home in Athens is known as ekistics; it takes its name from the Greek word for home. It calls for the closest possible collaboration between the technical and cultural disciplines, such as engineering and architecture, on the one hand, and the behavioral sciences and public administration, on the other. If such a science is ever to be evolved and applied, public and private interests must walk hand in hand.

The question of where responsibility lies thus points unmistakably to the proposition that the base of public and private cooperation must be broadened, and the local programs—either public or private—need to be put to work within the framework of the larger region.

Our third and last big question deals with involvement. Who is to participate in the necessary and countless programs of the future? This basic inquiry returns us to the fact that cities are people, but people increasingly alienated and dispirited—people who seem to be twice isolated, first by a ruling society which has excluded them, and second by their own feelings of intense alienation from such a society.

As we attempt to break through this twofold isolation, the principle of participation offers a key. In recent years, systematic studies of behavioral scientists have repeatedly demonstrated the positive force of participation in solving a wide variety of human problems—in arriving at complex decisions, in improving worker productivity or military morale, in breaking into the so-called poverty cycle, in rehabilitating delinquents, alcoholics, and addicts, to say nothing of deepening the motivation to learn at all educational levels. Such studies reflect the theory that the greater the involvement and the broader the participation of human beings in an enterprise, the more likely it is to succeed.

Only through some measure of participation can the alienated be brought into the mainstream of life and given a true sense of responsibility. Nor should we be unprepared for outbreaks of irritation, and perhaps worse, during this process. I feel strongly, for example, that even the picketing of schools by concerned parents, and rent strikes by aroused occupants of substandard tenements, can be healthy signs. A parent concerned about his child's education has broken through half of the isolation of the slum; he is concerned, not irrevocably alienated. I would suggest, consequently, that high priority be given to programs that stress participation by those who are to be helped. We should allocate more authority and responsibility to the poor to help both public and private leaders in the planning and implementation of constructive programs of all kinds.

The most basic issue of involvement centers on the racial crisis in our larger cities. Ghettos are characteristic of practically every American city. We know now that conditions which tend to keep one group isolated generate pressures that inevitably result in explosions.

In my judgment, businessmen must establish new and effective relations with those who have been isolated for far too long a period. People in Watts, or Harlem, or in the ghettos of Newark or Detroit, need to participate more fully in the workings of American business. We must invest money, time, and effort. And such investments can be profitable.

It must soon be universally accepted that all Americans are full Americans regardless of race, color, or circumstance. We must hasten progress to that goal by eliminating discriminatory practices in the building trades, through open housing legislation, through better educational facilities, and through fairer employment opportunities on all fronts. The seriousness of this issue cannot be overemphasized. Unless we resolve it, the American dream will evanesce.

J. Irwin Miller said this:

> Violence and disobedience are wrong and constitute a danger to the fabric of society; but it is also very wrong, and illegal, and contrary to our free country's dearest principles to keep any segment of our peoples depressed and deprived—simply because the white majority has the power to do so. Of the two dangers, the latter has usually proved in history to be the more formidable.

The question of who is to be involved may be summarized in one sentence: Programs must be designed and implemented with full participation by the people to be helped—irrespective of race, color, creed, or circumstance.

It is my conviction that the future is no longer a distant and irrelevant period of time. Our future is intimately involved in the urgency of the present. It is my further conviction that man is intelligent enough to undo the confusion he has created. If our social problems are great, so are our talents, our resources, and our determinations. Man's highest hopes, his greatest experiments in living, have been acted out in the cities throughout the course of history.

The city of the future will demand not just excellent physical design, but the conservation of human values; not just a comfortable conformity, but a vibrant diversity; not just a collection of special interests, but the setting for a truly democratic and proud community. This is the nature of our common dream.

Business and Demography: The Population Crisis

We live in an age of spectacular social change, and businessmen must be concerned not only with changes which directly affect their own businesses but also with changes which substantially affect the welfare of entire communities and the nation itself. Population change is a prime example. The Equitable Demograph display at the New York World's Fair continuously recorded a net increase in the population of the world of two persons every second. Such a rate of increase is potentially self-destructive and must not continue indefinitely. The demographic development of the human race has brought the world to the point where the rate of reproduction in any part of the globe affects the economic stability of the whole, to say nothing of the health and welfare of the rest of the world's population.

Delivered at a symposium of scholars on Population and Growth sponsored by the National Industrial Conference Board in June, 1966.

Since businessmen by definition are committed to the profitable production and distribution of goods and services, we are inevitably concerned with population problems and policies. I believe that many businessmen would agree that it is of very dubious moral acceptability or economic health for some countries to enjoy a high level of living while others fight a losing battle against deprivation and suffering. Our humanitarian instincts are aroused.

The businessman can no more ignore world conditions than he can hold himself aloof from the problems of the community in which he lives and works. He has an important stake in the complex relationship between demographic trends and economic development. It is consequently of first importance that businessmen strive to understand better the truth about the relations between population growth and economic strength and development.

Population has long been recognized as an important factor in any equation of economic development. But the theories are complex and often contradictory. A basic formula which I am advised that Professor Hauser often uses in approaching this question has a self-evident authenticity. The formula declares:

If L equals the level of living, with O the aggregate output, and P the population, then $L = \dfrac{O}{P}$.

In other words, the level of living cannot rise unless output increases more rapidly than population. There are, however, three subordinate factors of special significance in the relationship between *P* and *O*. These are:

1. The changing age composition of the population,
2. The supply of investment capital,
3. The availability of natural resources.

Let us consider each of these factors very briefly.

A high and growing birth rate in low-income countries, by generating a population with a higher and higher proportion of the very young, produces far more consumers than it does producers and thus economic development is effectively impaired. Approximately 40 per cent of the populations of underdeveloped countries now typically consists of persons under fifteen years of age. Thus, a continuation of high fertility creates a rising ratio of dependent youth.

This condition necessarily reduces savings and adversely affects the capacity of a country to generate capital investments in productive equipment.

It is discouraging to consider how the pattern of population growth in the world today serves to nourish the existing imbalance between population distribution and the distribution of wealth and natural resources. A recent study of the National Industrial Conference Board reported that, although the total income of many less-developed countries had increased at a faster rate than that of many industrialized nations during the last six years, the gap in per capita income between the two groups had actually widened.

The depletion of natural resources is an ever-present

influence which inhibits the development and expansion of a country's productive capacity. Per capita food production has begun to decline in many countries.

Some geologists see the basic problem of resources as a death struggle between people and salt, because of the pressure which increasing populations exert upon the limited natural resource, water. To be sure, nuclear-powered desalinization plants have been proposed as an answer to this problem; but even if these were to become economically feasible, scientists warn against the consequences of the amounts of atomic waste which would be discharged.

Let us now return briefly to a reconsideration of the stake that the businessman has in the problem of world population. He has, of course, a direct or indirect interest in world trade, in the balance of payments, and in the development of world markets. In addition he has an important stake in foreign aid, if only as a taxpayer. He feels deeply that foreign aid cannot be successful in the long run in raising living standards unless population growth levels off. Indeed, in many countries where foreign aid programs have been most highly organized, annual per capita product has begun to decline. As we have seen, the dollar gap between incomes in the developing and industrialized countries is widening.

The businessman sees the need for a broad-based and effective program for improving the level of living in various parts of the world. When we return to the basic formula with which we began, $\left(L = \dfrac{O}{P} \right)$, we clearly recognize that the population component is out of line.

To the extent that foreign aid permits the survival of millions of people, without actually raising their levels of living, we are engaged in an essentially ineffective, inhumane, and uneconomic enterprise.

Programs for the control of population growth, which are acceptable on moral, cultural, and religious grounds, are obviously indicated. And such programs should be devised and implemented without further delay.

Meanwhile, it has become painfully obvious that even moderate rates of population increase seem to exacerbate social and economic problems in our own and in other highly populous and industrialized societies.

One reason for concern is the fact that the labor force will continue to expand sharply for the next twenty-five years (quite apart from changes in fertility). By 1980, the U.S. labor force is expected to be in the neighborhood of 100 million people. It has been correspondingly estimated that we will have to produce over one million new jobs each year for the next fifteen years in order to absorb these new workers.

Quite apart from the ability of the economy to create new jobs, we must also take into account the effect of fertility differentials between economic levels. Many of the new workers will come from culturally disadvantaged groups. The established high relative fertility of groups enjoying limited educational advantages will continue to have a significant effect on unemployment. It is estimated, for example, that about 7½ million youngsters will have left school without a diploma during the 1960's alone. Increasing numbers of dropouts, in a labor market which is constantly upgrading its educational and technical requirements, confront us with a serious dilemma indeed.

Other "costs" of population growth are found in the rapid process of urbanization: slums and overcrowding, inadequate educational facilities, congested traffic conditions, air and water pollution, the deleterious effects of increased internal migration on intergroup relationships —just to list a few examples.

To ignore the problems of our cities, or to close our eyes to such issues as chronic unemployment or rising welfare costs, could well be the road to economic suicide. As businessmen, we must participate actively in constructive programs on all such fronts.

One point should be heavily emphasized. A rapidly growing population is not a necessary precondition for the continued development of our economy. A declining birth rate need not have an adverse effect on business. Although the traditional assumption in this country has been that a rapidly growing population leads to increased demand and hence stimulates investment, the analysis set forth above shows that rapid population growth may and frequently has operated to inhibit economic development.

If it is surmised that there will be developed a 20 per cent increase in purchasing power during the next five or ten years (certainly not an outrageous assumption), the effect on the growth of the economy would offset a considerable decrease in the rate of population growth. To be sure, rapid population growth in our own economic history and in the history of the western world in general seems to have stimulated economic development. But in these instances, unlike the situation in many developing countries, the man–land ratio was low and a greater population was needed to achieve the economies of large-scale production. Today, however, the situation is very different. We no longer live in a traditional frontier society. But we *are* living on an entirely new kind of frontier.

The American business system will continue, most assuredly, to be characterized and propelled by inventiveness, imagination, and enlarged appetites and interests. Mankind has thousands of unmet needs; and in the future it will learn to express and fulfill needs of which it is at present unaware. Increasing productivity to meet such new and diversified needs is the future to which we should look. Our economy no longer requires the stimulation of rapid population growth to keep it healthy.

In closing, I respectfully submit that business should never become so involved with statistics as to lose sight of the importance and dignity of the individual.

Whether we are talking about population problems here in the U.S., in the developing countries, or in the world at large, we must never forget that we cannot measure progress simply by aggregate statistics reflecting per capita living standards. We must also strive to see that each person is assured the opportunity to possess the ingredients of a full and satisfactory life. These include not merely the basic necessities such as food, housing, shelter, health, and education, but also those political, cultural, and spiritual needs that are fundamental to all men. Only in this way can we meet the need and responsibility of supplying moral leadership in a tormented world.

If we truly accept this responsibility and sincerely and

thoughtfully become concerned with the quality of life, we have no choice but to be also concerned with the quantity of life. Since we are coming to believe in the right to die with dignity, perhaps we will eventually espouse a comparable belief in the right to be born with dignity. It seems that we might well endorse the current proposal to add a fifth freedom—freedom of the right of everyone to make intelligent choices as to parenthood and the birth of children. Whatever may prove to be the ultimate resolution of this essentially moral question, we in the business community must work together with government and private groups to forge a common point of reference in this most sensitive area of human behavior. We must find a high and feasible principle which can be embraced by all people, regardless of economic or ethnic background and religious belief. In all probability we will not live to see this work fully completed, but we will know that it has been begun.

Epilogue

On December 9, 1969, just a week and two days after his retirement as chief executive of The Equitable, Mr. Oates delivered the principal address at the 31st annual meeting of the Institute of Life Insurance, an association of 170 companies which he served as chairman in 1964. Mr. Oates used the occasion not only to remind his audience of the essential nature of the life insurance business, but also to take a hard look at the future. He did so in terms of the industry's capacity to serve the changing social needs of all people of the nation. It seems certain that the ideas contained in this, his final speech as an insurance leader, will help shape the industry—indeed, all of society—for many years to come.—B.C.B.

A Retrospective
Look Ahead

Perhaps the most significant feature of the life insurance business is the common pride we have in that business and the sense of dedication we share in our determination to serve it well.

We recognize together that the one basic reason for the very existence of this business is the manifold opportunities it affords to serve others.

Deep within us we know that we are put here on earth to serve and that we find our greatest reward in the performance of service to others. Service is, of course, the underlying theme of the activities of our Institute and the activities of our individual companies. Indeed, all that we have to sell is the perfection of service, since our products (policies and contracts) are not protected and can be copied by all. We know it, we feel it, we try to live it. And occasionally we should be reminded of it. That is my purpose today.

There are, it seems to me, three distinct levels of service in which our businesses are inescapably involved. (1) Our organizations must have at the core of their being the desire to serve the larger community; (2) our organizations must encourage all of their individual members to participate in this same ideal of community service; (3) our organizations must serve in a human way the people with whom we conduct our business. I propose to comment on each of these three levels of service and in the light of these comments take a hard look into the future.

Business must serve the larger community if for no other reason than to earn renewal of its tacit license to operate. In the last analysis business must continually justify its social content if it is to be regarded as acceptable and granted the right to function by the people it serves. We also know that it is in our own interest to serve first the larger community. In the extreme, we see this interest placed in jeopardy as portions of our cities are subjected to riots and go up in man-made flames. As Franklin D. Roosevelt observed over a generation ago: "We have always known that heedless self-interest was bad morals; we know now that it is bad economics."

So we know that we must each contribute to the health, strength, and well-being of the community. We have recently given evidence that we intend to act more aggressively in the light of that knowledge. We have done so, most obviously, through the life insurance two-billion-dollar investment pledge to further the development of housing and job-creating enterprise in the inner city. But let me respectfully suggest, too, that all of our daily business activity does, in fact, serve the larger community. Our insurance and annuity services in times of great stress *do* help to maintain and support the economic security of the family and of business enterprise. Our investment services *do* help substantially to maintain and develop the economic strength of American communities large and small. Our employment practices, our training programs, the relative stability of our employment structures, *do* offer the opportunity for social and economic mobility to tens of thousands of individuals and families. Our daily work *does* offer the promise of creative participation to those within our ranks. To say that we could do more, to say that we *must* do more—as many of us, I am sure, say to ourselves each day—is not to negate or belittle what we are doing.

In this effort to serve the widest possible community, we welcome the collaboration and assistance of all individuals and groups. In this regard we look first to the members of our own corporate organizations and encourage all employees and agents to serve their own communities as they voluntarily choose. We do this not only because it is self-serving, although it is that, but also because the need is so great and because the highest rewards come to those who voluntarily accept responsibility to serve the welfare of their fellow human beings. Civilization perishes when the individual loses concern for the welfare of all. It is hard to believe that there are corporate organizations in this land which demand total fealty of their members—no outside activities of substance, no identification with community problems, no involvement with the controversial. We can be grateful that life insurance companies—to my knowledge at least—are not numbered on this dismal roll. I suggest that such a corporate posture is essentially destructive—destructive not only to the individual ideal of the "whole man," but ultimately to the corporation itself.

There is a process of mutual enrichment which takes place when the individual with corporate responsibilities becomes involved in public service. On the one hand, he brings to the public problem a managerial and technical experience which promotes a sound solution. On the other, he brings back to the corporation an understanding of the "real world" which is essential for the continued vitality and growth of the corporation—and which, on occasion, may be converted into fresh economic opportunities.

A small but meaningful example will suffice to make my point. An Equitable executive—who has nothing whatsoever to do with our investment function—linked up his interest in health care for those crushed by poverty to the need for a health facility in one of our major cities. He brought together our investment officials and the leaders of the National Medical Association, which is, as you know, an organization of black doctors; took a significant role in the discussions; helped iron out many of the details during months of negotiations; and finally had the great satisfaction of seeing Equitable finance a community health center. I submit that in this one act of service many benefited—the community at large, the National Medical Association, the Equitable, and, in terms of experiencing the rewards of service, the executive himself.

In this connection, please take note of a condition which, in our emphasis on community problems and opportunities, we are apt to overlook. That is our need to serve everyone with whom we come in contact as an individual human being. I am led initially to this concern, I must confess, by our growing reliance on—sometimes, I think, infatuation with—the machine, the computer. The computer has the power and purpose to serve man, yet it has the hidden power to control man if misdirected. Which way the scales will tip is still in debate, but fortunately the decision remains with man.

The machine can do many things—it can analyze, compute, store, discard, and transmit information. In performing these functions the machine can assist man to better serve the needs of individuals. But I submit that no machine will be able to share the family joy in a newborn baby, or listen compassionately to the deep concerns of an individual or a group, or assist in solving the problems of a young married man or woman, or reassure a widow, or comfort a pensioner, or guide a student. All of these human acts require a human sensitivity, a human participation. And whether that response comes from an agent in the field, a clerk at his desk, or from the person who presides at meetings of the board of directors, I say it must be encouraged, sought out, and established by our organizations. No policyholder or beneficiary should deal directly or solely with a computer. Men and women must be used to interpret and transmit the conclusions of the machine.

Our objective, then, is to serve the community, to serve it with individual human beings, and to serve it in a humane way. We are required to be engaged in community development because of the nature of our business. Our methods—because we are engaged in business —are economic. But our functions, through which we make our efforts tangible and effective, are under the control of and performed by human beings.

Let us now attempt to focus on the future—a future which is not at all certain, whose outlines are at best blurred, but whose coming must be anticipated and, as far as mortal capacity will allow, planned for. This, it seems to me, we can best do in terms of our basic and traditional economic functions—insurance and investments—as these relate to basic community development.

We instinctively recognize that man's first needs are biological and physical. We know that before he can begin to fulfill a creative role, he must have the reassurance of relative security, a feeling that he has in some measure control over his destiny. It is well known that our primary product, life insurance, promotes this feeling of self-sufficiency; that it is a taproot for the family tree and the well-being of society. Since we believe this to be true—and I think that most of us do—to the extent that we have failed to make it possible for all our people, regardless of economic condition, to participate in these benefits, to that extent we have failed ourselves and our purpose.

It is not inconceivable that the life insurance industry, its members acting cooperatively, might seek to join hands to help bring about a national community of concern whose single initial purpose would be the financial stability of those who constitute the so-called underclass of society.

Where should we begin—we who are essentially of a different culture, who presumably hold a different scale of values from those we seek to serve? Several avenues suggest themselves, but the one which appeals to me is within our own organizations—the thousands of people in our employ whose roots are in the communities we would serve. Let me remind you of a fundamental change which has occurred among the members of the traditional underclass—whether that underclass is based on race or economics. It is this: that the individuals are no longer content to seek only their own security; that even though they themselves are economically secure, their primary identity is with the group from which they came. For example, we have at The Equitable, as I am sure is true elsewhere, a growing number of black agents and sales managers. They are succeeding beyond our highest expectations. In discussions with them aimed at mutual understanding and appreciation, we have heard these men—strong men, for they had to be strong to succeed in a world which is fundamentally alien to them—express deep and anguished frustration with the impact on each other of our values and their primary identification with the very different communities from which they came. And we have psychologically shared a like frustration at our own inability to fully comprehend what they are feeling.

However, we must cling to the important fact that we have within our organizations rich resources. We must find successful ways to tap those resources. Indeed, the joining together of our two cultures—the middle class and the underclass—opens wide the possibilities for extended service to more and more individuals.

As the man of poverty needs a sense of security, in like fashion the man of affluence seeks innovative adventure. As our primary product has aided him in his rise to affluence, as it has provided him with security, it can now—through the innovative capacity of our organizations—provide him with a means of fulfilling in part a new adventure, an adventure of material means at risk, not risk of person but of surplus affluence.

We know that we can combine the two basic economic operations we pursue—the provision of insurance protection and the nourishment of the economy through the investment process. These combinations are of many kinds and involve modification of traditional concepts. We have already demonstrated this in variable annuities and in the concept of variable insurance. It now seems perfectly reasonable—even as the Institute's research has suggested—to extend our thinking a step further: to conceive, for example, a financial program which offers the individual client the opportunity to participate, not merely in the certain accrual of a death benefit, but in the venturesome accrual of an investment goal.

Given the technical capability within our organizations, we can now assemble and report vast amounts of complex data to our prospective client which permit him to select an investment goal and allow him to work toward its attainment at his own pace.

It is submitted that such a program offers to the individual an exciting and attractive alternative to mutual funds and direct stock market activity. By substantially expanding our products and thus our ability to serve, we also invite the exciting prospect of further competitive engagements where I am confident that we can more than hold our own.

Or consider our role as health insurers. Here, we are at once faced with a profound fact: Access to health care is now recognized as the right of every individual American. But we are simultaneously faced with an unhappy corollary fact, namely, too few Americans today are receiving adequate health care. I include not only the poor, not only those who reside in rural poverty pockets and urban ghettos, but the vast portions of the middle class, and I do not exclude some of the very wealthy.

We see the costs of medical care rise astronomically, yet we see no comparable improvement in the quality or availability of those services. We pour large amounts of government money into hospitals and medical care, yet we do not find concomitant savings or improvements for people needing care.

The fact is that this nation is facing a crisis in one of its most basic human services systems. It is a crisis which demands action and change. It is a crisis which challenges not only the health professions, but our insurance industry.

In my view, we must meet the challenge, if the health insurance business is to survive. And we may very well find, if we look carefully and innovatively, that the crisis also presents us with significant opportunities to serve both the public interest and also our business interest.

It is tremendously heartening to see the response of the health insurance business to this "crisis of opportunity." The action a few weeks ago of the Health Insurance Association sets a worthy goal for all in the health insurance industry by asking that we

> . . . formulate programs for, and exert leadership to achieve, a *pluralistic* system of health economics for this nation which will assure *all citizens access* to needed health services on an *equal basis* and regardless of the personal means for *payment*—making *maximum* use of *private* health insurance but recognizing that some use of *government* funds is necessary for persons of limited income.

This significant "call to arms" is based on recognition of the fact that financing is but one side of the coin of health care delivery—that while insurance has been principally concerned with funding, it must now give serious attention to the vital organization for the delivery of health care. Clearly, then, we have an obligation to act—institutionally and individually. The question is: How? Certainly there is no "one best way"; in the years ahead, no monolithic method for the delivery of health care, or its financing, can make sense in our pluralistic society. We'll have to move in many but coordinated ways.

Perhaps the most significant way in which our industry can serve the cause of adequate health care is by participating directly in its delivery system. We shall, individually and in the aggregate, have to seek the most appropriate roles. But it is conceivable that we should serve as the catalytic agent which brings together all groups with a stake in our health-care system.

Our life insurance industry could take steps in this direction right now. We could, for example, allocate a portion of our current inner city investment commitment—say a quarter of a billion dollars—to the financing of ambulatory care facilities. These "walk-in" neighborhood-oriented services are the number-one priority in health care delivery today. We could set the pace for America—and serve dramatically in the public interest as well as in our business interest. Here, too, within our organizations we find those resources of knowledge and responsibility which will allow us to get on with the job.

In sum, it seems to me that we should espouse the development of new types of health-care delivery systems which will contribute to the provision of quality care for all and take advantage of the resources of the private sector in developing, funding, and managing such systems.

Now, let me turn briefly to our investment function. There are two social situations demanding our attention. I refer, first, to the effects that our investments have on the surrounding environments, and, second, to the rising need for what traditionally has been considered high-risk capital and therefore not our concern.

We take pride in our role as the primary source of long-term investment capital, and rightfully so. The testimonials to that role are numerous and long. We should all be aware that we must continue to perform this most valuable service.

But we must also be aware of some of the possible and unfortunate side effects which some of our investments may have introduced. If we have made it possible for a manufacturer to build a new plant and thereby create new jobs, that plant may also have added to the pollution of the atmosphere, or it may have contributed to the new problem of thermal water pollution. If we have made it possible for a builder to construct a luxury apartment complex, that building may also have displaced numbers of middle- and lower-income people without providing replacement homes.

We must develop a higher capability to make sound judgments on these matters, and to make sure that our investments are not only sound, not only providing an adequate rate of return, but also that they are in the public interest. In the case of a highway shopping center, for example, we must be reasonably assured as to traffic conditions, as to the displacement and rehousing of people, as to the economic effects on older portions of the community, and as to the social effects on the larger community. We must, in short, be willing to condition our loan negotiations with social and ecological as well as with economic sophistication.

It might reasonably be argued that this is the function of government—that it is government's role to set standards for developments which affect the quality of life. And indeed it is! But if we have learned nothing else in this decade of the sixties, we have learned that government needs all of the thoughtful help it can get from private institutions. We have learned, in fact, that if government does not receive the help and support of its citizens, it quickly breaks down and becomes ineffective. Indeed, from the government's point of view, our experience as large institutional investors, operating in a national arena, brings us a breadth of knowledge which local governments need.

This leads to my second conclusion—that we should seek out wider opportunities for participating in the economic life of all underdeveloped areas of the country, particularly since we have seen our two-billion-dollar inner-city fund prove to be so highly beneficial. This has been the message for all of us who have pursued our shares of these pledges with flexibility and enthusiasm. Just think of what we have done: We have made it possible for literally tens of thousands of people to live in better homes; we have made it possible for thousands of others to find rewarding jobs within their communities; we have made it possible for hundreds of individuals to become successful entrepreneurs; we have made it possible for community groups and others to construct thousands of new apartments for as many families who previously lived in virtual squalor. All this we have done, and I suggest to you that our industry has known no finer hour.

If we are to continue to participate in the social revolution going on about us, then we need to cultivate a frame of reference—an attitude, if you will—which sees problems in terms of opportunities. We shall, I predict, develop a capacity within our own organizations to link up our resources—resources which are financial, managerial, and technical—with the opportunities which will inevitably be found in the communities we serve.

Somewhere, someone is developing a process which will save our rivers; and the insurance industry will, in ways yet to be discovered, make it possible for him to prove that it will work. Somewhere a child is wretchedly sick; our industry is working on ways to help provide the attention he requires and deserves. Somewhere a family is finding it impossible to secure an economic foothold; our industry must do its part to show the way.

Let me then conclude with this thought: Over the course of recorded history, the idea of restrictive privilege has slowly given way before the stronger idea of equality of opportunity. We are now obviously in the midst of a most exciting and demanding chapter in that history. Quite literally we are all given the great and precious opportunity to contribute to the creation of a more highly developed social order. At the core of this order is the ideal of service. Albert Schweitzer summed it all up beautifully when he said: "I don't know what your destiny will be, but one thing I know; the only ones among you who will be really happy are those who have sought and found how to serve."

Let us then seek new and better ways to serve—today and in the future. In serving, we shall surely find our fulfillment.

It has been a joy to be with you these twelve years and more. It has been a joy to work with you, to be inspired by you, to know you, and to care deeply with and about you.

Index

Robert K. Merton, educator and sociologist, is Giddings Professor of Sociology at Columbia University and, since 1942, has been associate director of its Bureau of Applied Social Research. He is a former president of the American Sociological Society and a Fellow of The American Academy of Arts and Sciences. A prolific writer, Professor Merton is the author of *Social Theory and Social Structure*, a modern classic in the social sciences.

Blake T. Newton, Jr., president of the Institute of Life Insurance since 1962, has led that organization, which consists of 172 member companies, into new areas of social and economic planning and action. Mr. Newton, an attorney, was formerly an executive with The American Telephone & Telegraph Co. and, from 1957-1959, was president of the Shenandoah Life Insurance Co. in Roanoke, Va.

Burton C. Billings is director of creative services in The Equitable's public relations division, and a former editor of its employee magazine. During Mr. Oates' tenure as chief executive, Mr. Billings had the opportunity to write extensively for and about him.

On December 1, 1969, James F. Oates, Jr., retired as Chairman of the Board and Chief Executive Officer of The Equitable Life Assurance Society of the United States. For the previous twelve and one-half years, Mr. Oates provided distinguished leadership of that organization and, during the period, was a strong influence in the entire industry. That influence was largely exercised through his public words as delivered in approximately 200 speeches. Three of those speeches were delivered under the auspices of the McKinsey Foundation Lecture Series, sponsored by the Columbia University Graduate School of Business, and were published under the title of Business and Social Change.

Mr. Oates came to The Equitable from the Peoples Gas, Light and Coke Company in Chicago, which he served as Chairman for nine years. Previously, for nearly twenty-five years, he practiced law in Chicago, latterly as a member of the firm of Sidley, Austin, Burgess and Harper. During World War II, he took a leave of absence from his law firm to serve as Chief, Purchase Policy, Army Ordnance Department, in Washington, D.C.

A native of Evanston, Illinois, Mr. Oates attended Phillips

Exeter Academy and served as a Second Lieutenant in the U.S. Army during World War I. He was graduated from Princeton University in 1921 and the Northwestern Law School in 1924.

Mr. Oates continues to serve as a director of The Equitable. In addition, he is on the Boards of Colgate-Palmolive Co., The Brooklyn Union Gas Co., The First National Bank of Chicago, and the New York Telephone Co. He has long been active in many civic, philanthropic, and educational organizations, including the Committee for Economic Development, the National Industrial Conference Board, the National Urban League, the Life Insurance Medical Research Fund, the American Museum of Natural History. He is a life trustee of Northwestern and a charter trustee of Princeton.

Following his retirement as chief executive of The Equitable, Mr. Oates rejoined his former law firm in Chicago as counsel, and he and Mrs. Oates have reestablished their residence in Lake Forest, Illinois.